FREE LOVE

# TRUE STORIES OF LOVE AND LUST ON THE INTERNET

THOMAS KELLEHER

east bay press

For further information please contact:
East Bay Press
4200 Park Blvd., #142
Oakland, CA 94602
www.eastbaypress.com

ISBN 978-0-9844329-1-2

Printed in the United States of America

Original design concept by Jon Whitman. Special thanks also go to Sean Harvey, Thomas Haughom and Ari Kahan for doing that Voodoo they do so well.

First Edition Printing, October 2010

www.tomkelleher.com

# INTRODUCTION

Nearly 40 million singles in America share a dirty little secret. They're using the Internet not just to surf free porn, steal music, and stalk ex-lovers; but also to find true love (and/or) lust online.

Birds do it. Bees do it. Doctors, lawyers and bored housewives do it. Why shouldn't you do it too and use whatever means are at your disposal to seek out that elusive soul mate, fall in love, or whatever?

Perhaps you already are, and you're one of them, but don't want to readily admit it. But why not?

The truth is that online dating has grown immensely popular over the past decade, due, in part, to continuing advances of the Internet and the proliferation of dating sites. And in shifting priorities in life, with less emphasis on careers and corporate ladder climbing, and more focus on living more enriched, fulfilling lives, seeking out companionship and/or developing meaningful relationships. The basic human need to feel love, or gratuitous sex you don't have to pay for, suddenly became more important than the need for obsessively monitoring the stock portfolio, that shiny gold Rolex or exquisite new pair of Manolos.

And so people started looking for love, but not in traditional ways – they used technology. Men and women alike spent less time going to singles bars and night clubs, hiring matchmakers, sitting through awkward dinner parties, and even more awkward singles events, and turned to the Internet instead, looking for love online. Mainly because it was there, it was new and it was easy.

After all, dating takes a lot of time, money and hard work if you rely on old school ways of meeting people. You have to actually go out, make yourself look presentable, and agonize over that perfect outfit, without looking like you're trying too hard. You have to work up your conversation starters/ice breakers/witty jokes/pick-up lines that never work. Line up your "emergency call" from the best friend for a quick escape should the need arise. Remember to set the Tivo. Fight for cabs. Shell out a week's income on overpriced watered down cocktails. And, of course, risk rejection and wind up going home alone anyway.

Isn't it more desirable instead to simply spend an hour surfing the Net, in the privacy and comfort of your own home, wearing the sweats you wouldn't be caught dead in with a glass of wine, and few expectations? A lot of people seem to think so. After all, what's the worst that can happen? You don't connect with anyone interesting and you go on about your evening with your Chunky Monkey, watching [adult swim] and you try again tomorrow. Your total personal, financial and emotional investment for the evening: nada. (Except for the ice cream.)

The Internet is truly one of the greatest innovations of the twentieth century and it has completely changed the way we live, work, communicate and interact. More and more people are using it all the time to meet others, make new friends, find love and/or otherwise hook up in today's ever-evolving, high-tech, wired world.

Yet, for a lot of people (especially those who haven't been initiated), online dating carries the same stigma that used to be associated with printed personal ads: that you must be some kind of desperate loser or social misfit to have to resort to placing a newspaper ad in order to get a date.

(Have you ever heard of Helen Morrison? The Helen Morrison? A little history: in 1727 Helen Morrison, described as a lonely spinster, became the first woman to place a "Lonely Hearts" advertisement in her local paper, The Manchester Weekly Journal. The mayor of Manchester immediately had her committed to an insane asylum for a month. Poor Helen. She was actually just looking for porn but got a straight jacket instead.)

Anyway, when you did meet someone from a personal ad, the first meeting was a blind date and you never really knew what you were getting yourself into until the actual date. Sometimes you got lucky and the night didn't end in tears. Other times you got a cross-dresser with "a few extra pounds" wearing a boa, who you swear could have been your uncle Steve that no one in the family likes to talk about.

But despite their shortcomings and somewhat risky nature, personal ads actually worked for a lot of people, and as a result, became more and more popular over time. It wasn't long before these classified ads would find themselves online, along with more structured "socially acceptable" dating sites, which at the time were very new and largely unfamiliar terrain, (unlike today, where there are over 1,400 dating sites in America alone).

While free personals were, and are still, considered to be the wild west of online dating, commercial dating sites offer a safer environment with professionally designed user interfaces, extensive personality profiles, ability to post photos that look somewhat like you (10 years ago), detailed descriptions, and the means to seek out others using very specific parameters, and additional safety through the use of anonymous emails. But not for free.

So daters have a choice. You can shell out thirty bucks or more a month in subscription fees in an attempt to stand out among the 40 million other online daters out there, and hope to find that perfect match. Or you can take a chance and get on your horse and ride on over to the seedy world of free online personals and give that a try.

FREE LOVE – True Stories of Love and Lust on the Internet documents this increasingly popular trend and presents a collection of actual online personal ads as they appeared and the stories behind them — all told in the posters' own words, warts and all, ranging from quite mild to very wild. It's real and it's raw. You'll laugh. You'll cry. You'll cringe and squirm a bit. Over five years in the making, these stories encompass a diverse range of people, economic and ethnic backgrounds, personal needs, wants and desires, sexual orientations, preferences and lifestyle choices.

It's about taking the concept of old-school personal ads – once shunned and eventually seen as an accepted way of meeting people – to the next level. It's not without risk though, and free can come with a price. There are scammers, con artists, prostitutes, and otherwise bad people out there trolling the personals looking to do harm. But there are also a lot of great, perfectly normal, non-desperate people out there too, looking for the same things we all want – love, lust, companionship, an apartment. You can find them all and have a truly rewarding experience if you're a little cautious and exercise a bit of common sense. Think with your brain, not just your naughty parts.

FREE LOVE salutes those glass-is-half-full adventurous types who are brave enough to shun convention, embrace technology, risk rejection, and use alternative, sometimes frowned upon methods of meeting people to help them find the like-minded man, woman, couple or DOM of their dreams. Or at the very least, someone warm to curl up with for the night. Some have found that special friend, lover, missed connection or casual encounter they were looking for. Others haven't been so lucky yet and are still searching, but remain optimistic.

So what's your Internet story? Are you looking for love? Or are you searching for something short-term in a size David Beckham? That boa-wearing Amazon is still out there as well. Log on and get some. And thank you Helen Morrison. Just look at what you started. ;-)

For Laura

"I AM QUITE INTO THE KINKIER SIDE OF THINGS"

MEN SEEKING WOMEN

# Honest Men Do Exist

I'm very honest and funny, outgoing and easy to get along
with. I consider myself a romantic. I love to cuddle and
show my affection. I'm looking for real magic - a pure,
undying love. Someone who is sincere, honest and faithful.
Do you exist?

66 I met an older woman online one day that turned into a free trip to Hawaii. She IM'd me in a chat room and we started talking. After about two weeks of emails and instant messages, she asked if I'd go visit her. I said, "Hell yeah," and gave her my number, but I honestly thought she was kidding at the time. Then she called me late at night and told me that my ticket was waiting for me at the airport. I had no idea what she looked like. I'd sent her my pic so she knew what she was getting, but all I knew about her was that she was older than me (she was 41 or 42 and I was almost 30).

Well, I called the airport and sure enough they had a ticket for me. So I jumped on the plane and winged my way to Hawaii. I arrived there and had no idea who I was looking for, but we found each other and promptly went back to her place.

It was working out pretty good to start with. She was gorgeous and the sex was GREAT. But (and most men think I'm crazy for saying this) she wouldn't let me work. So any and every time I needed or wanted something I'd have to ask her for it. She'd always give it to me, but I couldn't be a man and it was starting to get to me.

She made her money illegally so I ended up 'borrowing' some from her and took my ass back home. She told me that if I stayed with her for six more months that she'd buy my ticket home. She said all she wanted was for me to keep her bed warm, service her and work on her house. Of course, what she meant was that she wanted me to be her puppet. I'm not going to be anybody's puppet. So after about a month of this, I headed home.

This is probably my most notable Internet experience, but I've met other women (married and single) online as well – mostly in chat rooms.

I treated them all very well, but the main thing they loved (honestly) was my tongue. Especially the married ones. I made them feel like they were still wanted. I mean in a long relationship you gotta treat your woman like every day you're still trying to get her and not take her for granted. But many men don't appreciate this and neglect their women. And hey, I'm not going to say "No" if a woman wants to fuck, and it's not my fault she has to go outside her marriage to do it. Some of them I'd fuck daily if I were married to them. Their husbands' loss is my gain I suppose. So overall I guess I'd say that my experiences have been pretty positive. Except for the fact that I'm still alone. I'm still looking for that elusive woman who's sincere, honest and faithful. 99

# I want to take someone to Reno

I am going to Reno next weekend and don't want to go alone. So if any of you ladies want to join me let me know. Think of it as an all expenses paid trip for two, with the second person not of your choice. Leaving July 11th returning the 13th. (Oh, that's my lucky number.) I don't want to go alone, so if interested let me know. I'm 40, not too bad looking (ha ha) and I will be paying for everything. So this can be a fun weekend. Don't forget there will be some requirements.

66 Four people responded to this posting. One was younger than me by only a few years and looked like she could have been my mother, the other must have been so wasted, she kept asking me to remind her what the email was about. The next was OK, but lost interest. I ultimately met up with the fourth person for a "pre-screen interview" over drinks. She looked very attractive in her leather jacket, jeans and a low cut top. I also liked the fact that she wanted to kiss me, her great ass and her maturity at the time. While I wasn't looking for a specific age, I'm in my forties and never hid this fact. She told me she was twenty-two, and she acted very mature over the drinks. We chatted for a while and I broached the subject of the "requirements" from my ad, and made sure it was clear that there would be some payback involved. She was fine with that and we decided to make the trip together the following weekend.

Well, on the way to Reno the truth came out. She told me she was actually only twenty-one, going to be twenty-two. Not too bad, but then things changed rapidly. The maturity left the scene and that was that. We talked about all kinds of music when we met for our drinks previously and I asked her to bring some CDs for the ride up. She brought only rap and tried to really shock me, mainly with her music and trying to pick the rudest ones, which didn't have an impact on me at all. Her speech and mannerisms changed dramatically and she kept asking me if I had a problem with her being black, etc., (which I obviously didn't, otherwise I wouldn't have gone on the trip with her).

After that, we still had a nice time in Reno and the sex was good, etc., but this made things a little awkward for me and it just wasn't the weekend I was looking for. I was actually glad that I brought my laptop along and that was good reason to spend some time working. I just suggested that she go to the pool or do whatever she wanted for much of the time that we were over there.

We had sex twice – well, once full and one blow job in the morning. Otherwise, we went downtown (no pun intended), walked into a couple of casinos and had dinner at the hotel, but that was about it. I was a little fearful of taking her out much because I didn't want to see how she would act after seeing this other side of her personality. I think she was OK with the weekend, and she even sent me an email telling me she had a wonderful time. I was a complete gentleman the whole time. This was the first time I've looked for someone to go away with for the weekend. I'd do it again, but next time I'll put more specific age limits on it I think. I'm 45, so I think I would probably look for someone between 30-50, and really not over 45. I really don't act 45, but I don't act like I'm 21 either, so someone closer to my age next time would probably make more sense. 99

# Seeking Gold Digger

I have a question. What is wrong with materialism? I've traveled some and it is obvious that the SF Bay Area is one of the
most materialistic places on earth. So let us embrace this!
Why deny?

If all you want is money, or what it can buy, hey, bring it
on! I'm up for that. Let's get things together,
when we get together.

SWM, 140, 5'10, handsome, fun, free time.

" My ad was complete bullshit. It's part of a series of postings I've placed over the last few years. I think it is fascinating to watch people's needs and such change within online personals, especially ones like these – it's so anonymous and people are more honest. I post these ads to see what kind of response I get to various key words that seem to be holding people back from dating each other. I did get one response to this ad, a sweet woman who I had to ignore as I'm not 5'10" and handsome. I'm surprised though. I thought this "gold digger" ad would get more response.

I've posted many of these types of ads before. I once posted an ad that promised I would tattoo a woman's name on my butt to show my commitment (because women like commitment). That one got a lot of responses. My favorite was from someone who asked, "Do we have to actually date in order to get the tattoo?"

I see these personal ads as a form of expression and creative writing. It's nice to have an audience. Two or three years ago I also did very well dating from these ads. It was great to have a place online where people liked to write long letters. After a while though, it changed. I met some really, really crazy people and eventually stopped dating online as a result. It's very, very different now than it used to be. Now I just mainly use it for the entertainment value more than anything.

A large percentage of the personal ads I see posted are complete crapola. I don't just mean that they contain lies like listing your height as two inches taller, etc. I mean they're either fake or social hacks. As something of a social hacker myself, I know the following types of BS ads are very common, as my friends post them all the time. For example:

*Fake Females* – These people grab a picture from some other website (often a dating site) of a woman; a babe but not too much of a babe. Then either invent or adapt their own profile to support this woman and wait for the responses to flow in.

Presumably there are fake males too, but less I would guess. I've always wondered. The point of these ads is to basically see what sort of competition is out there, learn how to write a good response to other women's real ads so that you can stand out more, and to check your own ad writing skills judging by the number of responses received.

*Picture Collectors* – These become fairly obvious when you have dated for a while. These are people who are looking for nude and/or sexy photos of others to do who-knows-what with. Oftentimes, these photos wind up on other dating sites as fake ads, passed around on the Internet or used for "other" purposes. It's a good way for gay guys to get straight guys' naked photos, because they're more than happy to provide them to what they think is a hot woman looking for some extra curricular activity. If they only knew the truth! That said, my personal feeling (and this is all complete speculation) is that most of these ads are posted by women. I mean, they get so many responses (literally hundreds of them) and they know, quite rightly, that there are a great many sexual deviants on anonymous text-based personals. So I've always thought when you see an ad that says something like, "bitch dominant goddess – send me a picture so I may know if you can serve me," or something along those lines, then that's probably a woman filtering out perverts from her other responses. This makes it more of a different category from the picture collectors though. I've seen a posting where a woman actually admitted to doing this, so I know that there's at least some element of truth to this.

*Pervert Traps* – These are pretty obvious too and really a subset of the picture collectors. I've heard stories of people making arrangements to meet up with someone, and discovering that what they were expecting was much different that what actually turned up for the date/encounter.

*Quiz Ads* – These are not so much fake, but certainly belong in this list as they are essentially social hacks of collected information for many posters. Quiz ads are the only ones I sometimes still respond to 'for real' – often because I know a quiz ad is only to entertain, so there's no real pressure there, as it were.

So why is it that people don't seem to catch on? I can think of several reasons. Many simply don't care – it's a numbers game online, people send out anything. Or perhaps they haven't been doing this very long or reading the ads closely enough.

And you never know, it might be real.

# Sugar mama wanted

If you enjoy the finer things in life such as traveling, gambling, beaches, expensive jewelry, fast cars, fine dinning, Four Seasons, spending sprees, and taking care of a sweet sensitive 45 year young fella then this is it. I have no money and I am happy. You are sweet, reserved, and can get outta line in a fun type of a way. You are pleased to take me on cruises, vacations to China, Europe, Israel - almost anywhere in the World. I am comfortable in any country and am able to serve you in a manner above and beyond your wildest dreams. There are so many places that I enjoy, i.e. Europe, Piccadilly, Germany, France, traveling by BMW or modest van. When traveling, I enjoy photography and downloading our wonderful photos to a laptop computer where we can then have the most memorable days of our lives recorded, post carded or sent on to our near and dear friends.

If you have read this far, I applaud you. As for all you wonderful women I appreciate your input and look forward to your response. Please remember, if you work a regular job please press the backspace key now. If you are a women of heart and mind with >6 digits yearly income, your response is received in a warm way. Feel so inclined to attach a photo of yourself and something you enjoy doing and you will surely see me. Thou shalt bless thee in many ways.

" I normally don't place ads like this, but I thought it would be a nice change to meet someone who would be interested in having a friend or maybe even a little companionship, but most of all just traveling around, meeting people and having a good time without any strings attached.

I thought I would like to meet someone more financially secure then myself and basically go for a fun ride, providing there is an interest from both parties that it would be fun. As for romance, that would be an added plus. As for just meeting a new friend, that would be wonderful.

So far there haven't been any responses.  "

# Looking for an Online Affair

I'd very much enjoy a passionate, sultry, sensual, online ONLY
affair. The writing of deeply touching words, exchanged via email,
stirring loves sweet emotions to smolder within, creating thoughts
of equally tantalizing depth to course and ripple through us both.
The only requirement is...pure... unbridled...PASSION!

" I am a male transvestite and can be quite manly (rough, tough, etc.). However, I can also look and act female when I choose to do so, and am told that I do so quite well. I am androgynous, both in appearance and mind set. Some things I reason as a male would, others I reason as a female would, depending on the item at hand. I was born this way.

I've been married for twenty years. My wife is my best friend and is fully aware of everything I do, and outright approves/tolerates my activities and desires. She is a truly remarkable female.

I started writing on the Net for two reasons. First of all, I was in search of passion. After twenty years the passion goes out of any marriage, but thankfully the friendship remained in mine. The other reason is that I'm a writer (a poet actually) and I contacted others via the Internet in order to stimulate my writing. I've found many great muses out there, but one in particular is, and always will be, the *ultimate muse* for me.

When I first started with my Web search, I wasn't even sure what I was looking for, nor where to go look for it. My computer experience was nil. Zippo. I had never sat behind a keyboard in my life and although I'm a writer, the Internet was something delightfully new to me. For I quickly realized after a few short minutes of first accessing the Net that using it opened possibilities of real passion. Being a poet, I crave passion. I was in Heaven! I happened upon a "Web Girls" site for the first time and there, right before me, was an unlimited choice of every kind of female I had ever imagined. I noticed that most offered "free" areas and some with email contact possible. So I picked out a few who triggered inspiration and wrote to them. Most were very friendly, pleasant and kind, etc., but they were there to get me to join their sites as a paying customer. I wasn't there for sexual thrills, so joining any site would be a waste of my time, and not joining a waste of theirs. All were lovely, but whatever I needed remained elusive. Then one day, about two years or so ago, I randomly came upon a photo of . . . HER! I was instantly pulled deeply into her eyes, further than I ever imagined and felt feeling things I've never before felt. Never had my core been touched so . . . tantalizingly.

To say I was intrigued is putting it mildly, for I was *inspired*. Lines of prose shot through my brain faster than I could jot them down. I had to find out if I could write to her, so I pulled my eyes from her photo and visited her home page. This started what was to be the single most compelling and inspiring experience of my life.

She did have an email address so I wrote to her. Nothing of what I was feeling, of course. Just the usual guy things, commenting on her beauty, etc. She replied shortly afterward, seeming much like the others, but yet, different. I, of course, realized the "hook" was dangling and took most things she said in the context of her business procedures, but I continued writing her almost daily (often multiple times a day).

I asked if she might enjoy fantasy stories and she responded positive, so I began a series of typically lengthy erotica to her, putting as much passion into them as I felt. This went on for quite a while and our exchanges became more personal. She seemed to be opening up as much as I was and I began to send poems, which were inspired by her various photos. Very few of the poems were of a sexual nature, but rather what I saw while looking at the pictures of her nude form. She was stunning! But it wasn't her incredible body which stirred my thoughts, for her eyes remained the source of that which inspired me so deeply, and with each photo I viewed, prose came to life. There were many times that she had sent me a picture from her latest photo shoot, and within minutes a poem of beauty flew from hand, like the words themselves were born from her beauty, flowing like magic. This happened automatically and without thought with me just picking up a pen, putting it to paper, viewing the latest photo, and POOF . . . a poem was created! I had no knowledge of what words were coming from my hand. It seemed as if I was under a spell of sorts. Yet, when I looked down at the poem, or poems before me, it was my handwriting and the pen was still in my hand touching the paper. I know this sounds far fetched, but it's true. She could inspire things within me like I've never felt, and have never felt since. It was like our souls had kissed and love was spoken of often. While it may have in reality all been a game to her, it was real to me. She is the only one who knows whether she shared her real feelings, or was simply toying with me. 🙶

# Lonely in Upstate New York

I want a relationship with someone with similar life interests,
with good looks, slim, or not overweight is also important.
A relationship that does new and different things that makes
life fun every day, with commitment to each other, to share what
life has to offer and is going on in each other's mind without
getting mad, and to be able to keep private conversations to
each other.

OK look, I am being up front. I was in love with the mother of
my children starting at the age of 21 years old through life.
It was the best! I lived in Boston for 10 years then moved to
New York for a better job. While working all the time, she lost
the love in me and moved out and on. That was ten years ago.

Now since then life has been somewhat different as I have been
missing something/someone. So here I am, a man 43 years old and
dating again! Ha Ha. LOL.

66 This looked like a way to find someone new to start a new life with after my wife went astray and wanted a divorce. So I got a new computer and found this site and had a great time meeting new people. I have since found the one true love of my life with this ad and am getting re-married soon. My bride is coming to the United States from West Africa. She loves me so much and I do the same. Men and women have better luck finding someone from outside the country to come live with us and get married. I've found that American women want money and only what you've got, and from outside the country they want nothing but love and freedom. That is the kind of person that I found (or I should say that she found me). She is to arrive here some time this month if she gets her Visa.

When you put your faith in God, wherever on Earth he chooses to send you for a wife, you just have to have trust that he has it all planned out. It is our choice to accept what he sends to us. Personally, I put a lot of trust in God and think this is meant to be. I prayed to him every day to help me find someone that would be my partner in life, and he connected me with my new beautiful bride to be. When we chat with each other, it seems that we found the answer to each other's prayers to God to connect us to our soul mates for life. So now I am sending the American embassy two thousand dollars for her Visa so she can come to America to be my wife forever.

I am a man of forty-three and she is twenty years old and will treat me like a king here in America! They don't have anything there and when they come here, it's like heaven to them. They will never leave you like American girls do, who are spoiled with their wealth and money, hungry all the time and want the most expensive things and not the simple things in life like the Africans do.

It's not what you have – only who you are and how much you live your life that should be important.

Some people are calling her a mail order bride. But she is not. We met in the chat room and took it from there by sending e-mails back and forth to each other until I eventually proposed to her online. There are a lot of women out there that want to come to America to be your wife and they will do what you ask them because you control them. If they don't, you can send them back and they do not want to go back where they came from. So they are very loyal to you to keep them here in America, the land of the free. "

# Unique entrepreneur offers plum benefits

I offer the right lady a unique blend of humor, intellect, maturity, common sense and a fun-filled companion for scrabble, cards, sexy fun, hiking, biking, golf and more. I am very active outdoors and indoors. I am looking forward to having a companion to share the events of the day, including business. (I am developing a business and am looking forward to reaping the rewards of succeeding.)

" I have had considerable success with meeting women online. One was engaged to be engaged, another near engagement and there were various other tryst get-togethers. None from this ad yet, although I am currently talking to a lot of women from it. I am 63 years old, Jewish and am only attracted to black women. That is a problem in Oregon where less than 2% of the population is black, so I tend to look outside of my area to find people and the Internet helps me do that.

The ladies I got involved with were all single and available for a long distance relationship, so none of these were "on the side." They were all very nice, intelligent, normal people. One was a professor at the university I had graduated from in 1967. Rather ironic. She came out here to Portland from back east for about a week. The others were from Chicago, Dallas and other distant locations.

I was well acquainted with all of them from several months of emails and from lots of talking on the phone. And lots of phone sex. (Yes, even professors do phone sex.) These experiences were from 1998 to 2001. I had some medical problems after that which discouraged me from getting involved, but now I am healthier than I can recall in the last 40 years. When I meet someone online or locally a full spectrum of STD test results is my requirement to proceed with the relationship, No test, no sex. Of course all of the long distance ladies had the test and it was never a problem.

The professor was the best of the sexual experiences. She was toned and very hot. She, in fact, admitted to me that she didn't realize she was so hot as a lover. None of these relationships lasted all that long for very different reasons though. I would say the long distance effect was a significant factor. Any relationship is a crapshoot. My first two marriages were also from long distances, so I guess I had some early successes there – at least for a while.

As I mentioned, I am currently chatting with several black women as a result of this ad. Fortunately I have a very favorable long distance phone plan, and I can talk to all other 49 States, Puerto Rico and Guam for around $20 a month, 24/7. Heck of a deal.

Heretofore the long distance relationships I've had were all very normal, highly charged, and sexual in nature. I do far prefer sex with black women, but I get along with Catholic women the best. So I guess my ideal find would be to meet a black Catholic lady. Once I find her I will marry her for life. „

# Join me in Bali for a New Years to remember.

I have various business interests in Bali and speak fluent Indonesian. I'm a SJM, 38, 5'10", blonde hair, blue eyes, 188lbs, fit, & good-looking. I am a rare combination of book smarts, business smarts and street smarts. Add to that a sense of humor that's a cross between Robin Williams and Dennis Miller (and Curly). I'm extremely creative and have dabbled in the following professions: travel writer, the-ater critic, importer, retail chain owner, adult education director, non-profit executive director, graphic designer, copywriter,exorcist, general contractor, photographer, poet, marketing consultant, philanthropist, foundation director, industrial designer, herbologist and kabbalist/mystic. I'm accomplished, romantic, strong, witty, vibrant and, most importantly, silly. I seek a beautiful (in/out) spiritual soul mate between 22-29 who can keep up with me, be my muse, travel the world with me (I've been to 91 countries so far) and knock out a few kids along the way. She should be feminine and look good on the back of a Harley. If you're interested or have any questions, give me a holler.
-Beryl

I've been searching seriously for three months on the Web for my ba'shert (yiddish/hebrew for 'destined one') and have been misled down dozens of blind alleys going nowhere. Particularly frustrating is a repeated experience I call 'cyber interruptus' – after a positive exchange of an average of a half dozen letters, out of nowhere the woman sends a dear john email that she blah, blah, blah, bye. In one such experience, out of nowhere the woman accuses me of being a bullshitter, with a skeptical Astoria, New York, "You're a Rolls-Royce dealer in Bali. You support the Bali School for the Deaf. You plan to open a chain of gelato stands there. Pullllllleze. What do you take me for?" When I sent her proof of all this through my websites, instead of apologizing, she says, "You're too exotic. Bye!" There's no point writing her – she's a provincial mediocrity because these types of 'cyber teasers' love to have the final word and block my emails. One women's 'final word' was, "I am woman, hear me roar!" What a cliché.

I've also encountered again and again the frustration that ninety percent of the women posting ads prioritize that they want a man with a great/goofy sense of humor, and when they find one, they're apathetic. For example, as part of a letter I sent out as a reply to their ads referencing a GSOH, I said, "I've got two dragons holding a Yin Yang tattooed on my bicep. I also have the word 'MISS' tattooed on my penis. If you're the right girl for me, it will read 'MISSISSIPPI'. Put me to the test and we can at once ascertain my passion and your literacy level."

I had one response from a woman who took offense. Ninety five percent of the woman I sent this to (over 60 women) did not even respond. Only two others responded and said that it was hilarious. Conclusion: a woman who describes her sense of humor as 'goofy' is as serious as a heart attack. I don't think women know what they want. Based on my past experience, when they say that a good sense of humor is most important, what they seem to really want is:

a)      Security, security, security,
b)      Male model good looks  (even though they're common, average),
c)      Control,
d)      Someone to show off to her friends,
e)      Tall men ('if you're not at least 6' don't waste your time or mine'),
f)      If they're over 30 they want a baby, a baby, a baby,
g)      If they're over 40 they want the lost youth their ex stole from them, and
h)      A younger man,
i)      If they're over 50 they want any carbon-based life form.

As for this particular ad, I was perfectly serious about having someone join me in Bali for New Years. Some were interested, but the timing was bad.

I had a 'princess' type write me and said she'd come if I'd pay her airfare. I wrote back that I would pay for everything but, and I would take an escort type if that's what I wanted. She protested too loudly that she wasn't an escort. I wound up watching the South Park Marathon on Comedy Central . . . alone. But not unhappy, and grateful to God for my health and having my mind intact after a bad two year depression that followed my divorce.

Still, I persist and am determined to find true love through this abstract medium fraught with gold diggers, bullshitters and desperate single moms looking for a meal ticket. I've even entertained the thought of writing about my whole online experiences – but only if it's a success story where I end up with a young, beautiful, accomplished wife. Then I will write it as a 'how to' guide.

I am confidant that I'm not under any illusions and that I will absolutely succeed, despite these past three months of extreme frustration. In 1990 I won an ECHO Award – the Academy Award of Direct Mail Marketing. If anybody can pull this shit off, I can. 〞

# Perfect Man for the perfect Woman

I am 6'3", 34 years old, 180 lbs. Non drinking, Non-smoking, Non druggie, Totally disease free, Not fat, Not ugly, Not old, Not perverted (I guess). Looking for an attractive/ semi-attractive FEMALE for unadulterated, uninhibited FUN. (Yes this means you can have your way with me.)

You MUST be clean and legal! And enjoy a tall, healthy, normal male for YOUR benefit (willing to clean house, cook, go clubbing, give you hot sex without fear, etc. - whatever your desire is...even simply curling up and watching a good movie).

Examples of a Good Date: We rent a nice movie and kiss each other softly, passionately, and endlessly. Drive me up a mountain and beg me to give it to you from behind. Keep you warm all evening and have me cook you an omelet and bring you coffee. Decide I am the perfect man to fulfill your fantasy.

Bad Dates (NOT desirable): You pull a weapon on me and rob me/shoot me/take my wallet. Reveal you are a transvestite/a man. Tie me up and hold me for ransom (tying up would be okay I guess under the right conditions) and/or extortion.

This is VERY REAL and NO, I honestly don't think you will be dis-appointed. A reply will receive a picture for every picture sent or just write and say hi and tell me your thoughts/questions... I'll do my very best to respond open and honestly.

Happily and sincerely yours,

-Adam

**66** Unfortunately, though my ad generated a lot of laughs and indeed it was straight from the heart, the only response I received was from someone I already went out with. **99**

# I'm That Guy Nice Girls Say They're Looking For

27 y/o grad student (ready to graduate in May), mixed ethnicity, 5'11", slim but in shape. Back on the scene after a long absence. Looking to hang out a bit, no pressure, and no expectations. Up for anything, outdoors or in. Just wanna hang and see what happens, but not afraid of eventual commitment.

I could tell you I'm witty, smart, and have great lips — I do, but how would you know? Drop me a line. At the very least you'll meet an interesting person and possibly a new friend.

" I'm recently divorced and the prospect of meeting women again was intimidating. After all, I hadn't asked a woman out on a date for like five years. In the first couple months of being on my own I was depressed a lot and lonely. My ex and I had moved to DC so that I could go to school. I tried to spend all of my free time with her. The result is that I hadn't made any friends here. So after the divorce I was on my own, no wife, no friends, nothing. I didn't really have any way of meeting people.

Then one day I was posting an ad online trying to sell my car and decided to take a look at some of the personals. I read a few in each section (M4W and W4M), and was intrigued. I'd never done anything like this before so I decided to give it a try.

I knew I wasn't ready to really date yet and didn't

have much to offer in terms of a real relationship at the time. I just wasn't ready. I was also aware that I wasn't an amazingly good-looking guy, but a wiz with the personality. I'm not ugly, but I'm not the guy you notice from across the room either. I'm the guy you suddenly find yourself attracted to after three weeks.

I knew I didn't want to just go to random bars and try to meet people. Too much pressure. Besides, I wasn't looking for what I imagine people are looking for when they hit on women in bars, (namely, sex). I just wanted to practice talking to women. No expectations, no pressure. Truth be told I don't really know what I'd do if some woman wanted to have sex with me. After being with my wife for so long the idea of being with someone else is kind of scary.

I really am that nice guy women say they want. I'm smart. I read. I'm funny. I like to talk, etc.

Also, the mistakes I made in my marriage and subsequent divorce helped me re-examine myself and how I behave in a relationship. It's as close to a revelation as I've ever had. I believe that when the time comes for my next long-term relationship, I'll be a lot better at being a good partner.

Using these personals has given me the confidence to take the next step, and start going out and meeting women face to face. There's a great comfort in just talking to a woman and realizing that you can hold their attention and she's not looking around the room trying to find someone else to talk to. She's actually interested in talking to me. It's helped me to realize that when I am ready to start really dating again I'll probably actually be able to find dates. After my divorce my confidence was shot. Now, even though I'm still alone, I've realized that I'll be okay and that I'll be able to find love again when the time is right. It's a nice feeling. 99

# Still single

I'm looking for a special lady that wants to meet
the nicest guy in Las Vegas, who's honest, caring,
funny, witty and loves to show affection. Drop me
a line if you don't believe me -- you might just
like me.

I have a picture upon request. I hope you do
also.

" I met this lady online who told me she was 28, blonde, a fox, 36/24/36 and that she was in love with me. This was after we talked for two months. It turned out that she was actually a very overweight 58 year-old grandmother having sexual problems with her husband and wanted a younger guy to cyber with online, but didn't intend to fall in love with anyone. That was my first experience with online dating. Most recently I encountered a women posing as a girl looking to come to the United States who I found in a chat room. She told me her mother needed an operation and asked if I could cash some checks for her in the U.S., and send the cash to Nigeria so her mom could get this surgery done. Well, it turned out that the checks were fraud and I went to jail for it and now have to clear up the whole mess in court. Charges are pending, but hopefully they'll throw out the case or I'll at least get off with probation. "

# You are a scream...

I want to get a good alcohol buzz on with a hysterically
funny, endearingly rude, audaciously vulgar woman in a bar.
Or maybe something else with said type of woman. The cuter
and brainier, the better. Or, you can just ignore this ad
like all the rest I've posted.

66 Most online dating leads nowhere. People lie about everything for the most part. My favorite lie is gender. Have you ever gone out to meet a girl and then find out that 'she' is actually a guy? It's not fun. (I wonder if there are any gay men out there with a parallel tale.) Anonymity allows people to lash out in ways they never could in person. Otherwise the bar is raised so high that no one wants to be with anyone, but everyone is left lonely. This is laughable. My problem: at 5'8" I am considered 'short'. Statistically speaking, this is actually average. I wonder what it is about women that makes them want a man who is two heads taller than them, instead of slightly taller? It would help if more women were better informed that males over 6'2" constitute less than 10% of the U.S. population. THEN trim out the married, gay, HIV positive (or other STD), and disproportionately overweight, and they'd find out that this is a

very small portion of the total population. Yet, every other W4M ad demands that you be over six feet tall. By the time you get through the criteria filter, there is NO ONE LEFT.

This particular ad got one response. She was 45 (10 years my senior) and lives 50 miles away (or at least, not here) and the conversation ended abruptly when I told her I don't have a car. I don't want one; I live in the city. I would rather not spend any money on a car and inevitable parking tickets, endure traffic induced migraines, etc.

So here we are again; the evil that is most women in America. At age 15, you ask any girl what they like most about a guy, and they'll tell you that it's his car. And obviously, by age 45, (one would figure is old enough to get a car of one's own if one so desired) the answer has not changed.

It's no wonder that American women are said to

be the biggest environmental threat on the planet. I am inclined to agree. From a young age they are instructed that their role in life is to consume. The consumption patterns of Americans, and particularly white women, are wrecking the planet and causing the greater part of humanity to live in poverty. They simply do not understand this. So I only date Dutch, no matter how cute she is. "

# I Suck At This

What do you think about my ad so far?
Kind of boring, I know.
What can I do to spice it up?
Want to come over and get freaky?
(No, that's too pervish.)
How about...
I like laughing and having fun.
(Everyone writes something lame like that.)
Lets see...
I'm a Chippendale dancer.
(Nah, that's a lie.)
Umm...
Women think I'm cute.
(Too completely honest.)
Hmm...
I stare at myself in the mirror for hours.
(That's too weird.)
Geez...
I had a dream I was kidnapped by mimes and trapped in an
imaginary box.
(That's just way too out there.)
I suck at this.
Any suggestions?
I want to write something mega-cool so I can get emails from
awesome girls who are nearly as rad as me, a 26-year-old guy
who lives in the city.

**"** I write ads like this mainly for entertainment value when work is slow. I try to push the limits of the personal ad and use it as a venue for my humor, so it's a good creative outlet for me. But I've also had really good luck meeting women this way off the Internet. They usually like my humor from the ads and I can typically charm them enough through email that they already feel comfortable when meeting me. We usually have a really good time and sometimes it ends with sex, other times not, but often times there will at least be a second date. I've made some really good friends, had several short flings, and am dating constantly.

I can't really say what I'm looking for. I would love to find a special woman I truly connect with and would love to get serious with that person. But right now I'm dating, playing the field if you will, and I make it apparent to these women where I'm at as far as my attitude toward dating. Typically the women are in the same place I am, so no one gets hurt and we all have fun.

The first ad I posted was back in October. It was a satirical piece about how I wanted a psycho girl-friend. I met a girl, and three days later we were at my house. She had never given me a photo, but had described herself and the plan was that I was going to help her with a sexual fantasy. She want-ed to show up at a random guy's house (mine) and have sex with him (me). We decided that when we met, if we weren't attracted to each other we would say so as soon as she arrived. So she came over and was into me physically, so about a minute later I had her naked on my couch and we were having sex. (Safe sex that is.) I won't get into the details, but she was a really attractive woman and since then, I've found the Internet to be an extremely interesting venue to meet all kinds of people.

Surprisingly enough, I meet a lot of very good-looking, intelligent, stable, people this way. I've dated a few models, an exotic dancer, business-women, older women, younger women, etc., and all in all have had a really good time. "

# You're home reading personals instead of out living life.

And I am posting an ad.

Let's get together for a drink somewhere in North Beach. Send me an email and I will reply. Throw on some jeans and a comfy sweatshirt and head out. You don't even need to do your hair, just throw on a baseball hat.

Let's knock down a couple of pints on the patio at O'Reilly's or some other little dive in the area.

No head games, no photos and no BS. Let's just head out and do something random.

Your turn.

"I've had incredible success with online personals. Over the past six months I've experienced both the dark underbelly as well as the brighter moments of online dating. I've dated over twenty people and have had over a dozen hook-ups. This week alone I have dates booked with everyone from a 23 year-old Berkeley chick to a 41 year-old lawyer, and I have an ongoing thing happening with three different girls.

My online dating activities ramped up again after my marriage ended. My ex-wife and I actually met online through a dating site about three years ago. People would ask us who set us up, etc., and we'd tell them, "The Internet set us up." Before we got together, I met over seventy women from the Internet through that website and various online personals. It really was a great way to meet people.

After my divorce I found myself on the rebound and back on the Internet. San Francisco is such an online, wired community that you can't get a coffee or even go to the ballpark these days without having access to the Internet readily available. So this seemed like a logical way to start dating again.

I'm staying away from the paid dating sites this time around though because I'm not really looking for anything serious right now. I'm mentally not ready for another long-term relationship. One of the women I'm seeing right now (who responded to this ad posting) just got out of a seven-year relationship herself. So our encounters are just fun, low key and mainly physical with no expectations.

I find that a lot of women I've encountered are looking for LTR on the Internet though. Most of them who are my age (thirties) or a bit younger start pressing the screws very quickly early on, trying to see if you're marriage material or not – or at least long term relationship potential. If you aren't looking for the same thing, or are up to their standards for whatever it is they're looking for, they will quickly dismiss you. Which I find amusing because I'm always honest and up-front about myself, what I look like, etc., and what I'm interested in and looking for. I don't play games. But women online lie about themselves just as much as men do. One woman I met up with as a blind date told me that she was "slightly overweight." That's fine with me. I'm height/weight proportionate and don't expect all women to be supermodel thin, but I am attracted to people who take reasonable care of themselves and I guess I should have asked her to be more specific. Because when we met, she was more than slightly overweight – she was morbidly obese. She wasn't exaggerating, misguided or misjudged by a few pounds because she hadn't been on the scale for a couple of days. She just flat-out lied. Why she did that, when she KNEW we were going to meet in person, I don't know. I couldn't end that date fast enough. Not because she was fat, but because she lied to me. This sort of thing happens to everyone who dates online though at one point or another and it's become something I've come to expect when

I don't demand to see a photo beforehand. It comes with the territory, but that doesn't make it right.

But hey, looks aren't everything. I met this one girl who was really smart, attractive, fun, bubbly – she really seemed to have it going on. It was almost too good to be true. We met in the city for drinks. A while later, this group of guys come  into the bar and they all seemed to know her . . . a little too well. I found myself wondering just how much I would be shelling out for this date by the end of the evening. I still don't know what was going on with that whole thing, but I figured I was probably better off keeping it that way.

Then there was this other girl who was very attractive and had a nice body and all that, but she turned out to be a total freak-show-sex-fiend-carnival. Her whole life revolved around drugs (a lot of them) and some pretty weird sex. The drugs were just chewing up her brain and it became pretty obvious early on that this was going to get scary and end very, very badly, so it wasn't long before I asked her not to call me any more. This was weird because she came across well over email and the phone as being pretty normal.

Which is really the power of – and double-edged sword of – the Internet. When you meet someone in person for the first time in a bar, blind date set-up, or whatever, they size you up by what clothes and jewelry you're wearing, how good looking you are, what kind of car you drive – it's all physical and superficial and that's the basis of their initial impressions of you. With the Internet, you do it though words. You decide first whether you have anything in common through communication and make a mental connection as opposed to a physical one, and you either hit it off (or not) based on how you interact with each other. Then you take it to a next, more physical level and decide if you're also attracted to each other in that way, as opposed to the other way around.

Of course, there are always exceptions to this (like in the case of the total freak-show-sex-fiend-carnival chick or those who feel the need to lie to you), but my luck overall has been better with people I've met online, than those I've met otherwise.

Here's a good example (and a major reason why I turned to the Internet in the first place). Back in my twenties, when I was visiting New Hampshire, I was hanging out in this bar across the street from the fleabag hotel I was staying in. This hot girl comes in wearing a black cowboy hat and dark sunglasses and sits at the bar next to me. (This was at night by the way, and the sunglasses should have been a tip-off for me to run.) I start buying her drinks and we both loosened up a bit as the evening progressed, but she wouldn't take off her stupid cowboy hat and glasses. Eventually she said that she was supposed to get together with some friends and invited me along. I was feeling quite drunk at this point, not to mention horny, so of course I went along. We drink more over the next few hours and wound up back at her place (both very drunk at this point), crashed on the couch, smoked a little weed, started making out, groping, and disrobing (including the hat and glasses finally). Her roommate comes home, and starts yelling at us for being somewhat naked and messing around on the couch in their front room, and so I suggested we go back to my hotel. On the way out, she makes a point of grabbing her friggin' cowboy hat and dark glasses. (This was around 2:00am and it probably should have been my second clue to run, but when you're drunk and horny you don't really think about those things.) So anyway, we arrive at my cheap hotel room and in no time we're quickly at it again, the clothes are coming off and all is going according to plan. We're getting hot and heavy into it and all of a sudden she tells me, "STOP! I need to borrow one of your ties for my hair." I thought this was a little odd, but oh well. Of course I get her a necktie to hold her hair up. (I wasn't going to argue with her at this point.) We go back to it, and I'm beginning to be really glad that I got her that tie, and she stops abruptly again and shouts, "OH MY GOD! I HAVE TO GET OUT OF HERE!" She grabs all of her clothes and runs out the door half naked – she didn't have any pants on but made sure she was wearing that stupid hat and dark sun-glasses – leaving me sitting on my bed, scratching my head and wondering what the hell had just happened.

So now when I'm starting up a dialog with someone new that I just met online, you can probably imagine what one of my initial qualifying questions is going to be. And if you ever find yourself in New Hampshire and run into a girl wearing a black cowboy hat and dark glasses, at night . . . don't bother. 〞

# Guy with nice butt seeks girl with nice butt.

I want to date a girl with a nice ass. That is all really. I'm not incredibly picky about what you look like or whether or not you even have all your teeth. As long as you have a nice butt, then we'll probably get along. Who knew dating could be so easy...

" I won't bother with the "nice butt" ad again. Women seem to be very sensitive about their asses. "

# Cum help me fold my fitted sheets.

Here's the deal. I hate to fold fitted sheets. Something about the billowy nature of the sheets, combined with the elastic, makes these sheets less than ideal for folding. If they were a perfect flat square or a rectangle, no problem. You could just fold them -- bingbangboom -- like a napkin. But the fitted sheets? Hell no. They always seem to end up in a ball in the closet.

Ok, so here's what I need. I need YOU to come over and help me fold my fitted sheets. And then have sex with me.

You: kinda like Martha, only not quite as frumpy. Have that stuck-up, WASP-y "I know everything about everything" attitude that she does. Also, have that subdued, insider-trading bad girl streak that she has as well.

Be as confident in your ability to give a blowjob as you are in your ability to fold fitted sheets. If you can pull off saying, "Oral sex. It's a good thing," after giving head, that's a big plus. Be as horny as a Chow-Chow in heat.

Me: I'm tall and thin, in decent shape...and badly in need of someone to help me fold my fitted sheets.

66 I received one serious response to this post from a woman who got stood up that night. As a result, she said that she had a bad attitude and was horny. She told me that her friends call her "Martha" as a joke because she loves to decorate, cook and be a control freak.

She sounded great. She described herself as 5'10", fit, athletic build and recently left women for men because she realized she liked the dick more. She went on to say that she was very sensual and knew how to please people, and herself. She told me to drop her a line if I was interested and tell her more about myself.

This sounded promising, and so I did. But wouldn't you know it, no luck. I liked the "bad attitude and horny" aspect of her email, but alas, this just wasn't to be. 99

# I might be short but I am unique.

Hello. I am a 4'9 dwarf and this is not a joke either. I was born a midget. I AM OK WITH WHO I AM. I just moved to Boston from L.A. I am working as a consultant for a new up and coming production company. I am successful, well-dressed, business savvy and educated. I am told I look just like Joey from the show 'Friends' but of course a lot smaller! LOL. I am looking to meet a nice girl who is open minded enough to see "below" my physical attributes and get to know the 6 foot handsome gentleman I am on the inside and to be friends first and see what can pop up from this friendship, if anything at all! I am looking for a girl who is healthy, attractive, but obviously not flawless (how hypocritical that would be). Please be 22-34, I am 26. I hope I can meet someone nice. Thank you and good luck to everyone.

66 No one responded. I cannot get a break! I hate that I was born this way. I try to love myself, but it's just is too hard. 99

# I need a huge favor.

I've got a dog, a Dachshund, which I really, really love. His name is Champion Von Hoffmeister Wilhelm von Birchbeinstamer, or "Willie" for short. He's really cool, too. He's the roommate everyone wants to have. He'll chill on the couch and watch TV with you, smoke out with you (he comes over and starts licking the bong, so I blow a little smoke his way), and he's just cool to hang out with. The craziest thing about Willie is that he TOTALLY gets off on porn, while you're watching porn, too. I've recently decided that this is not healthy for him though. See, Willie is a Champion Doxy, which means that he's a top dog. Other owners want their bitches to mate with Willie and they want him to sire their litters. Well, when it comes time to perform, Willie wants none of it. And it's not because he's into other boys. He just doesn't get the concept of "doggie style." I think it's from watching too much kinky porn.

So, what I need from you is to come over and let ME do YOU doggie style, so that Willie can see that it's OK for doggie style to happen. In fact, we need to do it doggie for a long time in order for Willie to understand this. I've found that Willie really digs 18-24 year old women, too. I know this because one time I left a copy of Barely Legal sitting around, open, and I found Willie scooting all over the picture of a comely young red-headed woman named Logan. He snapped at me when I tried to take the magazine away from him, so I know that he REALLY, REALLY digs the 18-24 year olds. So, if you're cute, 18-24, want to meet a friendly, mellow, cute little dog (nothing kinky with the dog, just me), and you want to smoke out and do it doggie style for a while, let's hook up.

Do it for Willie.

❝ I received one response to that ad . . . actually two. One was from someone who asked, "How do you know that Willie doesn't like redheads?" and the other was the following:

Hi....
I really liked your story. Can you make one up about a mermaid?
....That is, if you take requests.
Thanks,
Laura

Well, I did. I made up an ad involving a mermaid:

### *Mermaid needs lover for aqua play!! - w4m*

*When I was a kid, I used to look at the mermaid on the Chicken of The Sea can and think, "Damn, she's fiiiine." Everything about her stirred something in me. The golden hair, the inviting smile, even the tail! I wouldn't eat anything but Chicken Of The Sea. Not BumbleBee. (Are you kidding? What does a bee have to do with tuna?) And certainly not StarKist. First of all, I couldn't get over the dumbed-down product spelling ("Kist" instead of "Kissed") and second; Charlie the Tuna seemed desperate and creepy. With his glasses and those big lips, he just reminded me too much of the uncle whose lap I never wanted to sit on at Christmas time – if you catch my drift.*

As I got older, and became wise to the ways of man-woman intimacy, it was not only the picture on the can that turned me on, but also the SMELL of the product inside the can that turned me on as well! I'd open the can and just dive in; MMMMMMPPPHHHH – no fork, no spoon, no nothing. It was like I was going down on that mermaid on the can! Sure, I cut myself on the jagged edge once or twice, but it was worth it. Oh, it was insane! You know how you can open a can of cat food – any can, for that matter – and hear a cat hit the floor running from three rooms away? Well, that's how I was with tuna! Open a can and I started thinking about the first time I went muff diving. Go to a deli where someone had ordered tuna salad and gangway! I 'd make a dash for the bathroom in order to "work out a few issues."

Where is all of this going? I finally hooked up with a mermaid, and she is fiiiine – quite a catch! She's got a totally hot face, and killer tits with nice, perfect nipples that she covers up with scallop shells when company comes over. I can't give her what she wants, though. She needs a guy who can satisfy her. I've tried, but failed. We used to try conventional sex, in a bed, but it just doesn't work. The moment she approaches arousal, she starts flopping around like a fish on a pier.

Her tail starts flailing, and she flops off the bed and starts breaking shit around the house. The property damage from this is into the thousands and the risk of personal injury is just too great for me to bear. She needs a man who will hop into her tank *with her and excite her until she starts spewing her roe like a sturgeon. Think of how salmon don't actually HAVE a position, but just sort of rub on each other and turn all red and shoot their respective loads. This is what she needs. Do you want oral? She gives a mean underwater blowjob because she can hold her breath for so damn long! This will be one experience you won't forget! Hit us up if you'd like to play!*

Several things happened. One, I was flooded with email from guys. Guys, guys, guys. And a woman. She was trolling for sex for her boyfriend.

The other thing that happened was that I started a semi-serious email correspondence with the woman who asked if I could write the mermaid ad. Well, it turns out that she was a total tease, and stopped e-mailing me when I sent her a picture of myself. (I'm not a bad looking guy.) I think that she was actually like 17 or 18 herself, and, along with friends, was posting ads soliciting dick pics from 50-year-old guys. How do I know this? Around this same time, a woman posted an ad apologizing because her daughter and her friends were posting bogus personals. Several of the responses to my Mermaid story, as well as some of the weird stuff that happened when I e-mailed "Laura" ("mailbox full" sorts of messages) made me suspect that "Laura" was either the daughter or one of her friends.

And so, what did I end up with? A mailbox full of email from guys who wanted to screw a mermaid. "

"I WAS ALSO CURIOUS"

:-p

WOMEN SEEKING WOMEN

# Femme And Beyond

I'm a down-to-earth lady. I enjoy nature, dancing, antique
shopping, reading, exercise (walking), museums, spiritualism,
and cooking. I also have a passion for home improvement
projects. Personality-wise, I consider myself to be
passionate, faithful, honest, approachable, fun loving,
affectionate, and supportive. Physically I'm pretty: slim but
curved, romantic brown eyes, sensual lips, and a welcoming
smile.

I'm seeking a woman who is warm-hearted, NICE, down-to-earth,
and willing to communicate. Physical appeal is a good thing,
but character and personality are paramount to me.

" I'm not sure that the Internet is the best way for a woman to meet another woman in all honesty. Lesbians – or rather, quality lesbians – are extremely difficult to find. But it's quite easy to come across a bitter lesbian.

**shrugs** "

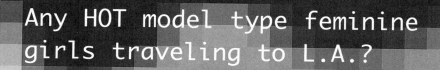

# Any HOT model type feminine girls traveling to L.A.?

HOT L.A. model seeking girl to play with, maybe hit Vegas or
Mexico. Let's sip drinks on the beach, giggle, flirt and kiss.
Prefer first timers so we can explore and enjoy! NO MEN,
couples, butch, lesbian etc.
Please send current pic and description and let me know when
you are planning on visiting L.A. so we can meet!
XXOOX

" I am in my late 30's and most of the girls that answered my ad are 22-24, so there is a huge difference in priorities. Plus they don't have much money to do anything. I guess women my age have five children and just clean the house all day? I haven't really had anyone other than a 31 y/o write me, but she had both arms covered with tattoos, and to be quite frank it, scared me! I have small tattoos, but she was a bit much!

Other girls couldn't send a pic, or they'd give me a number and I'd call, but they'd never call back. There is a lot of frustration that comes out of the whole process as it takes a lot of patience to sift through the fakes and flakes. But if you are bored like me, married, and don't have to work, then it is sometimes worth it (at least it's something to do) to maybe find that one girl or two with nothing to do either! "

# Not again!

Looking once again. Or is it, still looking? At any rate I am an intelligent, happy, attractive gal with a great mind and heart. Hoping to meet a femme for a possible connection. I seek beauty, intelligence, heart, passion and commitment in a gal looking forward to the future. Hope to hear from you soon.

" I am a forty five year old lesbian. Due to a back injury ten years ago, I have limited outside contact with people in social settings so I decided to try the Internet personals, online scene for about three years now to gain the chance to meet new folks. I placed ads and filled out the profiles on many sites and added a recent photo when and where I could and waited for possible responses. I was pleasantly surprised that I did indeed get many of them. Unfortunately, they all had the same theme, or deception going if you will. No one was as they described themselves.

I met many women that sent photos that were years older, or described themselves in a very wonderful light when they were in fact none of the things they described. I was simply horrified to learn that the "average" online person is nothing like they present to others.

I chatted online for a few weeks to a gal who described herself as follows: "blond haired, blue eyed fantasy gal involved in the motion picture industry. Educated, independent and head of the department."

Naturally I was intrigued enough to invite her to dinner out. What arrived was shocking! She was approximately 5'4" tall, and weighed about 210 pounds. She did indeed have blond hair and blue eyes though. During the dinner conversation, I learned that her motion picture industry was a photo shop, and that she was a shift supervisor of one other employee!

I did finish dinner with the gal, declined any drinks or further conversation and said my good-byes. My "fantasy gal" was still a fantasy!

Perhaps I expected others to be as I am; forthright

and honest, for I have no reason to lie to anyone. I want people to like me, not some image I portray. But, it has simply been a disappointment.

I do continue to try to find that one honest individual out there. But, thus far, I've had no luck. I don't think it is the appearance part that is the most disappointing factor when realizing the truth about an individual, but the integrity factor. The fact that someone would so willfully be deceitful when the chance they could be found out says little for the type of person they are. Perhaps they don't truly think others would notice the discrepancies, or even worse, perhaps they themselves do not. Oh well, I'm keeping fingers crossed and an open mind. "

# A fem that is searching for that special butch who will treat her right!

I'm a very down to earth, honest, loyal fem LESBIAN, with a good head on my shoulders that knows what she wants out of life and out of a life partner. That is what I'm searching for, a life partner. If you're a lesbian that is looking to just play head games I'm not up for that. I'm very mature. I'm only 18, but sometimes I seem like I'm 30. Everyone has their days to act young though I'm sure. I'm starting college in the fall, I took a year off to find myself and travel a bit. I've done that and now I'm just ready to settle down somewhere and get my life started. I'm planning on majoring in college to be a teacher for grade school because I love children, and I'm minoring in massage therapy. I love the outdoors, to ride horseback, have fun. Not much on partying but I do have an occasional drink once in a while. I'm looking for a butch, who is sweet and will love me for who I am. I know who I am and I want someone who knows who they are and are tired of these immature head games of, "I love you but I'm not in love with you." I like people taller than I am (5'7"), who aren't too "big" in size, but that doesn't necessarily matter... I can fall in love with someone for who they are. But be honest people - you have to have some physical attraction, even though to me the personality means more than anything, there still has to be that spark. I don't like bi girls who like girls but want you to join in with their boyfriend or another girl or just having a fling. I'm tired of flings and I want someone who just wants me... If you think you can deal with that then message me, I'd like to hear from you. ;o)

"I've met quite a few people over the Internet and have tried several online relationships before. However, in my experience, it's about the same as meeting people in person, except you get to know more about that person before you meet them. That is, of course, putting your trust in that person and believing that they are telling you the truth. I have met people who have not told the truth, and also those who are the trust-worthiest people I've ever met in my life. Two of my more memorable experiences are as follows:

In December of 2002, I was contacted by a woman who claimed to be a lesbian as myself and seemed as though she was decent, and greatly compatible with me. We talked on the phone for about seven hours the first night that she had e-mailed me, and the next day we planned on meeting. She drove from Kentucky to Virginia to meet me. From the day we met we had an instant connection (or so I thought).

She stayed with me for a week and after that time, we got the money together and planned to move in together. I lived with my father at the time, and it was my first time ever moving. Immediately, I felt unsure about it as I really didn't want to leave, but according to her, if I loved her, I'd do anything to be with her. I did move in with her, and it was honestly one of the worst experiences of my life. It has helped me grow up tremendously. However, if I could take it back I would definitely consider it.

I lived with her for three months. She had a daughter, whom I fell so much in love with – she was like my own child and I couldn't have loved her more if she had been my own flesh and blood. She is really the only reason that I stayed as long as I did.

This woman, who seemed to have everything together, really did not at all. She was a liar, a rip off . . . and now thanks to her I owe so much in debt and I don't have the money to pay for it. She was abusive, verbally and physically, and blamed everything on me. She was a really hateful person, she wouldn't let me work, but complained that I never put anything into our household, when actually I was the one who kept it running. I cooked, kept everything spotless, waited on her hand and foot, and took care of her child. While she was at work I had to stay put and talk to her on the phone the entire time. The rest of the time while she was home I had to watch her child, clean and cook, and after doing all that I basically got no time to do anything other than take a shower. I rarely got any sleep, but if none of that was done it was constant abuse. I stayed longer than I should have because I loved her baby and I didn't think she was fit enough to take care of her.

When we would go clubbing, she would make me drink with her and do drugs, when really I'm not that type of person at all. I'm a basically homebody and I want a family; not any of the other stuff that went along with her. The first two weeks were the best ever, but after that everything went downhill. She tried to make everything out to be my fault. About three weeks before I left, she cheated on me. She wanted me to have a threesome with her, and so I did, willingly, but was at the same time disappointed because what I had thought would be the best thing in my life had defiantly became the worst thing. The next weekend, she left me without money, food, or any transportation in a lot of snow and bad weather to go be with her new girlfriend – the girl we had had the threesome with. I was going to have a friend come visit me while she was gone because I really hate having to spend nights by myself, especially in a place I'm not familiar with. She told me that she wasn't allowed, and if she found out that she came over that she would kill me. I was going to leave that weekend (everyone told me I should) but I didn't. I really should have.

I waited on her hand and foot, cleaned the house, took care of her child, had her food ready in the mornings and when she got home from work. Basically I was her slave, and if I didn't do something just right she would either complain, get really mad and argue with me, or say that I was just using her, when in reality she was the one that was using me. ”

# Does anyone know where I can meet some cool studs?

Over the weekend I went to Blackout and met some cool-assed women. I met one named #$%^# but I think she has a girl. Anyway she was hot.

" I met this chick at a club, but I only got her name because she had a date with her. I was very attracted to her because she had a great smile when there was nothing to smile about. She was this beautiful black stud – really masculine – but beautiful, and very friendly. I really wanted to try to find her afterwards and meet her. I thought this might be a good way because I'm always browsing the personals and I've actually met a cool-assed friend online. I'm fairly open about using this forum to meet people, and although I wouldn't necessarily want my mom to know, all my friends do. Some of my "gay" friends will meet women online but none of the straight ones, because it's easier to meet the oppo-site sex in person than it is to meet the same sex . . . for obvious reasons. And I see that other people use it as a way to contact others so I posted this ad about her. I thought it might be a good idea to include her name (just in case) since I knew it and didn't want just anyone to respond. I was completely SHOCKED when I got an email from her. I called my friend on the phone (one who was there when I met her and had to hear about how much I was digging her for 3 days!) as I opened the email and I would have screamed had I not been at work!

Her "date" was the one who got her to reply to me. I met up with her at the same club and took her home with me – something I never do and will never do again! There was instant chemistry between us though and I was curious about her sexually. She was all stud, and studs will not usually let you please them. So for a feminine woman to get a stud AND be able to please her (or at the very least touch her) is like winning a prize. She was very open to me touching and pleasing her, which was great! She was very sexual and passionate and I was (and I'm sure she was too) in an infatuated haze. I thought I was falling in love with her, but I'm sure now it was just the sex! This went on for four days. We watched movies, ordered in and had lots of sex . . . until I had to go back to work. She came over and started unloading all kinds of intimate details about her painful life, which also had me a bit freaked out and afraid for my own safety and belongings. I realized that I didn't really know her and had no business being that intimate with someone I had just met. That's when I decided to end it. I broke it off immediately but she wouldn't go away. She called and came by unannounced, cried and everything. I eventually saw an ad placed for a butch type that said something like, *"Are you a sexy young stud?"* It fit her to a T! So I responded and told the woman where she could meet my friend/her type. IT WAS MY BUTCH'S EX/DATE that had initially hooked us up! We exchanged a few emails and decided never to let our butch know what happened! The butch and I still keep in touch, but I never agree to see her. What a mess.

I have had more positive experiences online, though equally bizarre. I was browsing the free ads for the first time and saw the w4w section. One ad caught my eye for a woman wanting to have her first lesbian sexual experience. I was also curious, so immediately I was attracted to this woman. She was about three years older than me and had grown up in the same area, even attended high school with my older brother, but she swore she didn't know him. I think she was really terrified that someone would find out about us! We e-mailed each other all day long, and would write about all the things what we wanted to do to each other sexually. The emails got to be too much and we agreed to meet. She told me her first name and I told her my nickname. When I gave her a call and said my first name on her voice mail, I didn't hear from her for two days! I tried calling her again, but I realized that I have a very unique name and that she must know me from somewhere after all! So I asked her not to "out" me to anyone since it was obvious that she knew people I knew. She agreed and said the chances were too great that we'd be found out and that we shouldn't talk again. But the attraction was still very strong so we met anyway, had amazing sex, and continued to have sex with each other over the next two years. It turned out that she usually goes by her middle name – which is why I didn't realize who she was – and she is best friends with MY best friend's sister! We've never met until we met up for sex, but have heard one another's names mentioned frequently. To this day neither of the sisters know that we are bi-sexual, but we have admitted to being friends. They know that we call one another, but we're able to play it off only because she is in a field of service and I was able to act like a client of hers. 🙷🙷

# Come play with me

I'm friendly, happy, easy-going, and adventuresome - come play
with me!

66 I have met a few people through the Internet that have been interesting (and entertaining) to talk to, although the very few that I have actually met with in person have been rather disappointing, for various reasons.

One woman I met presented herself as someone with a very sad past, who had overcome many difficulties, but appeared to have come through them all with the attitude of a saint. Of course I took what she said with a grain of salt, but even then I wasn't prepared for the reality. In truth, I'm still not sure what reality is for her, but as far as I can tell she is a pathological liar playing on peoples' sympathy to get free room and board. She was playing several women at the same time, and unfortunately for her, she chose a friend of mine to play also. When she told my friend I had seduced her, and persisted in pressuring her until I had my way with her, my friend knew things weren't right, and called me to talk about it. (I'm not pushy when it comes to sexual matters, and my friend knows it.) So we started to do a bit of research and found that most of what she had told both of us was lies. That was the end of that.

Then I met a woman that sounded like someone I would really enjoy getting to know, but it turned out she was married, and couldn't quite bring herself to make the leap from hetero to bi. She was just communicating her fantasies online and really was a nice person, but was not comfortable moving forward, with even friendship, when she knew I was interested in her physically. And then I met a delightful woman that I really enjoyed getting to know, but our age difference bothered her too much. (She said I made her feel old!) She was 16 years older than I am, which I didn't really mind, but in the end I guess it mattered to her.

I'd love to find someone that is honest, understands herself, enjoys some of the same things that I do, is intelligent, has a good sense of humor, enjoys getting physical and doesn't live too far from me. Will I find her here? I really doubt that now. I was aware of the dangers of online communication and I knew that many people lie here, but I really hoped this would be a good way to find what I was looking for. I don't really believe that anymore. It does seem, honest or not, that most of us here are looking for the same thing. But perhaps the fact that we are looking here at all says something about an inability to connect with people in reality. I don't exempt myself from this, as I have not had any more luck in the "real world" finding what I am looking for than I have in cyber space. Still, it's interesting to chat with people from around the world, and yet it's sad to see how many of us have emptiness in our lives that we are struggling to fill. 99

# Cute Italian woman needs sexy female for fun & more!!!

I am a 25 year-old Italian woman. I am 5'2", medium length dark brown hair, black eyes, and told that I have a great body, that I am pretty and sexy. I am not conceited; it's just what I've been told! Apparently I look like Sandra Bullock but I don't think so!  I have a lot of different interests and I'm always up for trying new things! Some things I like are reading, dancing, music, movies, animals, creative writing, and tons more!!!

I would love to meet a caring, fun and loveable lady  to have good times with. I love women. I love everything about how a female looks, to being able to talk about everything that guys just don't understand! I am very sexual and loveable. I would love to have a friend with benefits, maybe more. You can feel free to ask me anything.

"I've placed personal ads on a few different sites to find a woman companion. However, in the process of looking online for females, over a year ago I wound up meeting the man I am marrying next month. I had broken up with yet another boyfriend and was just learning about the Internet and heard about these dating/personals sites and decided to try it out. I got a lot of responses and went out with some guys that turned out to be real jerks. Then I met my fiancé, "James," who is shy and never talks to women. But he took a chance and contacted me and was surprised to see someone in the same city as him on the site. So he e-mailed me to say, "Hi." I wrote back, we met for a date and things just progressed from there. Eventually he proposed and we're getting married in September.

I have also met women through these sites, but no one I would care to see again. I don't know how I could do things differently. I put up the best photos I have and try to write as interestingly as possible. One very aggravating thing is the amount of men who have selective reading. I have an ad to meet women because I am bisexual and now that I have my man, I am looking for a woman. But even though my ads specifically say NO MEN and not to bother writing, you wouldn't believe the amount of responses I get from them. They seem to think they can change my mind or something. I've had to block several of them because they kept bothering me. I know other women who regularly have the same problem, so I know I'm not alone here.

I was interested in one girl from Vermont but she was pretty young (I think she was 19 or 20) and pretty immature, so we didn't talk much. She was also pretty much only interested in talking about sexual stuff, and I was looking for more than a party girl. More recently, in the past couple of weeks I chatted and then met a woman a bit closer to me from Massachusetts who looked different from her photo. She turned out to be a lesbian instead of bi, and was all over me the minute I walked in the door. I think she sensed I was uncomfortable with her approach since I haven't heard from her since then. I am chatting to one woman from the Boston area but she seems a little flighty, and she doesn't drive. And I *hate* to drive, so we are trying to arrange a time when we can meet – it just hasn't worked out yet.

I was bi (openly) for about three years before I placed the ad looking for women, so it wasn't really to explore or anything like that. I've had girlfriends before, but it's just really hard to meet women (as a woman) in normal circumstances, so that's why I decided to try the personals. But it's been hard to meet quality women this way, too!

My boyfriend/fiancé, by the way, is completely fine with me being bi. I had a girlfriend when I met him. I'm looking for a woman for a totally separate relationship. James has never been involved with a threesome and has no interest in doing so or even watching. (I guess I got lucky.) He has no interest in being with anyone but me, and he says watching is pointless – like watching a porno, you get nothing out of it for yourself! So the relationships are kept separate and it's good like that.

Women do need to be careful about who they meet though. I once met this one real creep whom, about fifteen minutes into the date when we were just walking through a park and talking, started asking me extremely personal, very vulgar, sexual questions and was being belligerent. We hadn't spoken on the phone before, we just e-mailed back and forth a few times and decided to meet. We were walking and talking and out of nowhere, he started asking me if I did anal, how many men have I done at one time, do I like women, do I swallow during oral sex, etc. I didn't answer any of his questions. Instead I called him a bunch of names and told him that he was ridiculously ignorant. Luckily, we had taken my car so I drove him halfway to where he was parked and kicked him out and told him to walk. When I got home from that nightmare, I e-mailed him and told him off some more because I was so shocked and pissed off about his obnoxious behavior. After I stuck it to him in the email, needless to say, I blocked him too. 99

# Have You Wondered?

Have you ever wondered what it is like being touched by a
woman? I am now wondering that myself and would like to explore
the possibilities with another woman, who is mature, and
discreet. Desire a friend as well where we can meet, shop, and
laugh as well while exploring this side of our personalities.
Ethnic background, & size is unimportant, as long as you are
d/d free and clean with a pleasant personality. I am married,
you can be too, but my husband is not involved. Let's exchange
e-mail and pictures to see if any chemistry is there.

" I originally got my computer several years ago thinking that I would use it to get organized, keep the household bills in order, manage my finances, correspond with friends, family, etc. Well, that did not come to fruition and it really became more of a play toy for me than anything.

This is my very unhappy fifth marriage after being widowed three times. The third marriage lasted for eleven years and we are still friends. My current husband has had a lot of health problems since day one of our marriage, which is something I was not aware of until after the fact. Being one not to give up or fail, I have struggled with this for twelve years now with no sexual involvement or emotions of any kind for a long, long time. During the course of this marriage, I can count on my hands the number of times sexual fulfillment has taken place. I just fell out of love right after the first five months of marriage. I rolled with the flow, left once and stayed gone for three months and was made to feel guilty about leaving, so I came back to him in Nevada.

Finally I discovered through talking with some acquaintances, the world of online personal ads and decided to "fool around with it" to see what would happen. Well, you would not believe all of the loveless people out there – both men and women. I would say there are more men than women, or so it seems anyway. I discovered that the majority of the people online were looking for companionship, and friendship, and if sex occurred, that would be an extra for both concerned. I also discovered that there are lots of flakes out there and one just has to be able to identify which are which, usually telling so by chatting a few times and being able to ask the right questions.

In doing this, I also discovered there are a lot of couples that desire threesomes, whether it be MFM or FMF. Upon chatting with some of these couples, I think it awakened something inside of me called curiosity. I made several attempts to try this, but each time I backed out for whatever reason. I have no idea as to why.

During this learning curve, I met a fifty-year old local man and we began a short-term affair of four months until he began to feel guilty (he was married). Afterwards, I met a thirty-something man from Europe who had come to America to become a citizen and we shared several sexual adventures together. He had different feelings regarding sex and he was much more open and understanding about the topic than people in the States generally tend to be. He and I once again entered upon conversations regarding a FMF relationship, which he said he wanted.

I had again balked at this, but at the same time I found myself still intrigued about it. We still see each other once in a while and have become very good friends.

Computers and the Internet have provided this for me – friends and acquaintances from all over the world, including someone from Holland, who is coming here to visit with me soon. We have sustained our chats for over a year now. Also, I've established a good friendship with a gentleman from back East, who is coming to Reno in two weeks. Assuredly, I will safely go to bed with these gentlemen and they will return home and we'll continue to be good friends.

So, having said that, I started looking on my own to explore the other possibility of looking for just female acquaintances to see if perhaps there is anything to experiencing another woman's touch. Bi-curious is all that it is; I adore men and their kisses, being able to protect us under their wings and cuddle us when we are sad or happy and being the one to give us such wonderful children, of which I have several. I am not sure I will act on this, but I have been told that I am a very good-looking woman for my age and I can still seem to be able to attract younger men and women.

So while this particular ad is fairly new, I've already received a request from a couple to form a threesome who live right here in my area. I'm not sure how I am going to respond to them either. I'll probably correspond with them to see if there are any common denominators there besides lack of, or want of, sex. Hopefully we'll establish an ongoing friendship and I'll eventually work up the nerve to experience the sensual loving touch of another woman that I've been curious about for so long. 99

# Lipstick Domme seeks Sub

I am a beautiful, elegant, intelligent, dominant bisexual
girl who is seeking her other half to feel whole. You are an
intelligent beautiful submissive who seeks the same.

There is no better time than the present...

“ I am a beautiful, confident woman who knows what she wants. And I always get it. Right now I want another beautiful woman to be my little love slave. I already have a husband, a submissive boyfriend and a host of admirers who enjoy the pleasure of my company. But I have this little itch that needs to be scratched, and so I posted this personal ad to try to find a new playmate that could complete me.

Finding men is easy. I get approached all the time by cocksure males hitting on me, using their pick-up lines, thinking they're God's gift to women and wanting to have their way with me. I find this both amusing, and at the same time, insulting that they think that I'm going to be that easy. They don't have a chance. Mainly because I like to be the one in control and doing the hunting. I'm naturally dominant that way. If you're a man, the way to get me is to let me come to you and be prepared to spend a lot of money. I like nice things and I expect you to give them to me.

But finding a quality woman, who is beautiful, sexual and intelligent is usually much more difficult, because they play too many games, are usually fake and often conflicted when it comes to sex with another woman. Unless they're lesbian, which I'm not attracted to (I like men, I like cock – lesbians don't, end of story), they just don't know what they want, whether they're straight, bi, lesbian or whatever, and get confused. Especially when you add BDSM into the equation. It's typically more than they can handle and they get scared away and flake when it comes time to actually meet. For this reason, I generally stay away from "bi-curious" or "first timers" because I don't have the time nor the desire to "teach" people anything (except for how to please me).

I want to be with a woman who has experienced another woman before and who knows what she wants. That may sound strange when you take into account that I'm looking for someone sub-missive. But the fact is, weakness is not a part of it. Submission is not about weakness. It's about willingly relinquishing control – total control – compromising, and trusting the other person completely to do whatever they want to you. Being the goal-oriented taskmaster that I am, this is much more intimate for me than the actual sex act. Anyone involved in the BDSM scene will probably tell you the same thing.

The funny thing is that there are a LOT of people out there, men especially, who are more than willing to submit to a beautiful girl at the drop of a hat. Sometimes all it takes is the batting of eyelashes or the possibility of sex, no matter how remote that might be. Ninety percent of the men out there with 'honey-do' lists and driving mini-vans with their wives and children in the back fall into this category. Do you think they really want to be living that life every day? Of course not. But they do those things anyway, willingly, because it's easier than arguing or putting up a fight. I can work with that. Men are like puppies. You need to spank them when they're bad, and reward them when they're good. And they love you all the more for it.

I've been active in this lifestyle for over thirteen years now. My husband is aware of all this and doesn't ask any questions. He's not interested in BDSM (only vanilla sex) which is somewhat boring to me and only touches on part of my sensuality. So I look elsewhere for it and get it. My boyfriend also knows, and I have the freedom to do whatever I want as long as I take into account the emotional distress it may cause him.

As his top, I'm responsible for his physical, emotional and mental well being. It's a huge responsibility, but one I take very seriously. So it's because of this and his potential hurt feelings that I'm focusing more on meeting woman right now to play with and using the Internet and tele-personals to find them.

But no one else knows, nor would they have any reason to suspect, some of the things I get up to in my private life or that I'm even bi-sexual. Not my family, close friends, church group, yoga class, colleagues – no one. Unless you've happened to be one of the lucky few to be tied up by my ropes, wear my training collar or experience my expert skill with a vibrator, to the rest of the outside world I'm just another "normal" everyday, happily married, church going, thirty-something year-old women living in the suburbs. Which is just the way I like it. I am all of those things, and much more. It's my own delicious little secret. 🙶

"BEEN THERE, DONE THAT"

:-C

MEN SEEKING MEN

# Dark Alleys

Don't know why, but I'm in the mood to bop around with a guy (preferably on our bikes), stop into some alleys, get off, get back on our bikes, ride some more, stop again...

Of course, if you live nearby, we don't need bikes - we can just walk around and get nasty. Anyone out there (NEARBY*) who's into this? Wanna' do it right now?

*Nearby means 94110, 94107, 94114, 94103

I sincerely believe that the Internet has replaced the gay bar for m4m promiscuity. Since mid-February, I've had 58 different men for sex. Of these, all but three were online hook-ups. Of the 55 that were established via online, all were through postings like this one. I can only guess that I've seen about a third of them a second or third time, but in most situations, the second encounter is the goal. Usually, folks' schedules (including mine) delay the process of meeting a second time – which is a fundamental reason that this works best for one-time encounters.

Of the 55, I am now currently dating one man whom I would NEVER have met in the waking real world – and I consider myself quite fortunate to have him in my life.

Out of all of these men, only four have been unpleasant experiences (and on an A-F grading scale, I would rate them a C- or D+). Although these figures are 'guesstimates' (I DO remember all of the 58, but I'm sure I've forgotten a few others), I could only guess that I've engaged in sex as a result of the Internet since February (when I returned to San Francisco) probably close to 100 times when you include "repeats."

The convenience of online hook-ups is quickly becoming the modus operandi for most men I know, promiscuous or prim. There's no loud, obnoxious music to shout above, no overpriced cocktails and (usually) a guarantee of mutual orgasm with someone you will probably not regret encountering on the street the next day.

Personally, I'm not into trying to flirt with drunken men who are surrounded by a gaggle of their less-than-pleasant friends. I'm not into second-guessing what that handsome man will do in bed. And I'm definitely not into collecting phone numbers. Been there, done that, have the t-shirt, gave it to Goodwill, saw someone else wearing it.

But, let's face it: meeting someone whom you find attractive in a public setting does not allow for the sort of questions that should take place before taking off one's clothes. Using the Internet, all the basics can be addressed in an up-front way – top, bottom, versatile, oral, anal, fit, average, stocky, positive, negative, bareback, safe, rough, age, height, weight, size, photo attachments, face links, "g-rated" pics, "x-rated" pics – it's all right there. If you do this the right way, it's very efficient.

Online sex cruising is no different than online shopping. If it's there, it's to be had. I've become quite adept at avoiding long, fruitless nights on the computer. My general rule is that if I can't find a sex partner within 45 minutes of signing on, I stop and call it a night. (Try that in a bar!)

In bars and clubs, we temper our behavior for social acceptance, often "dumbing down" our true sexual personae.

In contrast, shielded by anonymity, the Internet allows the inner pansexual to do the flirting. I, myself, have lived out a few fantasies that I would never have dared before and this allows people like me a forum for broadcasting these dirty little desires.

Although I didn't get the extrovert I had hoped to find from this posting, I did get a great bike ride out of it. The man, close to my own age, was a great conversationalist and was quite fun in bed. Unfortunately, his exhibitionism wasn't as strong as my own.

As I write this, I'm on the prowl right now. I'm checking posts online, seeing which pervs out there are as hungry as I. Each day, I allow myself to unearth a piece of my own sexual being; something that got suppressed through the years. I still want to attempt a number of "scenes" and experiences too wild to probably print here. All this will happen in time. Maybe even with you. ""

# A Little Drunk, A Lot Horny

Did Pride. Going to a party later. Right now, looking for a little afternoon diversion. I come over to you and get you off, or we get naked and let our hands roam and play. Would especially like it if we were outside in this great weather, but indoors is fine. Nearby is essential.

You/Me: The kind of guys who would never wear a rainbow shirt, emblem or logo, but identify 'queer.' NOT clean-cut. Prefer >35 <45.

" That ad produced the sexiest man in his forties I've ever seen. Pecs as hard as rocks, firm jock legs, furry chest and a passion that scorched me. "

# Do you like hairy guys?

I'm a 29 year-old male looking for some fun. Me: brown hair, brown eyes, goatee, 6 ft tall, 215 lbs, and very hairy. It's been a long week. Looking for someone to hang out with and play.

" I would say that I found exactly what I was looking for. I met some weird people and met some great people that will probably be my friends for a very long time. I posted the ad looking for new friends and, quite frankly, sex, because I wanted to rediscover my sexual side.

I found both. "

# Great catch for the right guy

What's up? My name is Scotty -- gold eyes and short brown hair, thin goatee, Italian/Irish and span 5'9, 160 -- open to whatever comes out of getting to meet someone. OK for physical to more serious if it comes to that -- not into the bar and club scene. Like sports, nature, travel but I am also a homebody type.

I'm looking for young guy, 20's or 30's in decent shape, average to good looks, masculine, straight acting type, regular guy, into talking, getting together and taking it from there -- wherever it leads -- who's open to taking the time and the chance.

" I was involved with someone for eight and a half years. After it ended and I was ready and interested in meeting some new people, I initially started placing personal ads in the Village Voice, etc., which also had voice mail personals. I never owned a computer before I started working at my current job, but before long I found myself in front of a new laptop and a whole new world. My co-workers knew that I was gay and were aware of some gay dating sites and introduced me to them. So I decided to try them out while still continuing to use the other personals and phone ads.

Each medium has its pros and cons, and obviously with the Internet you have the opportunity to see people's photos, etc., and theoretically see who it is that you're talking to, which can add or detract from the attractiveness or chemistry you're feeling with that person. But chemistry over the email, the telephone, and especially in person, are very different things – especially among gay men. A lot of gay men have a very specific type that they're looking for (usually physical). The way you wear your hair, your clothes and the color of your eyes have to be just right. And if you don't fit their type *exactly*, they say that there's no "chemistry" upon meeting you in person. Even though you've gotten along swimmingly through your correspondence or telephone conversations. Dating in the gay community can be so superficial.

Here's an example. I posted my online ad and included several recent photographs of myself. They were real photos, recently taken and accurately represented who I was and what I looked like, and included my face, body, etc. I'm an attractive, fit person and I have nothing to hide. Someone contacted me in response to my ad and he told me that he liked how I looked in my photos. We exchanged emails and chatted on the phone before making plans to meet up. Because he's from Queens and I live in Brooklyn (a fair distance away), I offered to meet him somewhere halfway, but he wanted to get together closer to me. He wanted to come to an area that he was comfortable with and frequented all of the time, and catered to people of his same ethnic background. Upon our meeting I could tell instantly that there was something wrong. He was cold and distant and not at all as friendly as he was before. We eventually went back to my place and he said he wanted to use the bathroom. He raced in there and practically slammed the door in my face. This guy wanted to meet me based on my photos (he *told* me that he saw them and liked how I looked) but was still obviously disappointed upon meeting me in person – you could see it on his face. Then all of a sudden he started complaining about the distance and making it into a big issue, etc., (even though he comes here all the time) and making excuses for why he should leave. He obviously had a problem with how I looked in person. I don't know what it was that he saw that was different than my photos (which he said he liked), but now I go into a lot more detail about what I don't look like than what I do, in order to try to avoid similar nasty experiences. I've had more than my share of experiences like this, especially from the print and telephone personals.

But the online personals have their other problems too. A lot of people (and I'm still talking specifically about gay guys here) really aren't whom they claim to be and/or are evasive – like they're hiding something or are playing around on someone. Some people like to go around and around with emails and string you along for long periods of time that never result in anything. I don't mind exchanging emails 2-3 times to look for someone, but I eventually want to exchange phone numbers so that I can talk to them and get a better sense of who they are. Email is just too impersonal. But there are lots of people who are reluctant to do that and only want to IM, etc. One guy told me that he likes to do that to screen out the weirdos, but how can you do that by only exchanging one-line messages? Others just keep asking for photos and keep sending IMs. Who knows where those photos are winding up? And this is from a legitimate dating site, so why are these people so reluctant to phone or meet up? They *must* be hiding something.

A lot of them are involved I think. I got together with a few (supposedly single) guys who would get all possessive with me and want me to remove my ad posting, etc., so they could have me to themselves. But then after a while they'd become evasive, call me at weird times and then disappear after a few months and I'd never hear from them again.

Then there are the "curious" types who don't know what it is they want. I met this nice guy named Mark (not his real name) from this ad. We saw each other every weekend and did a lot of fun stuff together. We'd kiss and hold hands but he never wanted to stay over at my house or be intimate. We made plans to go away together to Florida for a little mini-vacation and he was preoccupied with how many beds were in the room. (This was after we had been dating for a couple of months.) Everything was set and when it came time for me to meet him in the city at the train station to go to the airport together, he was supposed to call me when he was about to leave. He never did. I called his house several times and there was no answer. I had him paged, and still no answer. The next day, after still not hearing from him, I called the hospitals. I was relieved to hear that he wasn't registered anywhere. I finally got his mother's number and found him there. He became angry and said, "We need to talk." Mark went on to tell me that he didn't think that he should be with anyone right now. *Nice*. This was after he let me buy the plane ticket, book the hotel reservations, etc. He said he'd reimburse me for his half of the expenses, but when he did his check bounced and I eventually had to take him to small claims court (which he never showed up to). I won the judgment but spent the next year trying to collect from him.

I never really found out what was going on with him, but I was feeling quite hurt, rejected and vulnerable from all of this and really needed to get away from it all and try to forget about everything And I wanted to meet someone new – anyone – to help get my mind off things. Florida was still looking good to me, so I started looking for someone who might be interested in going away with me for the weekend. My friends joked that I'd probably wind up with some axe murderer or something and be found dead in my hotel room. So anyway, my travel date was approaching and I finally meet this guy online who sounded interesting. We chatted back and forth, exchanged photos, spoke on the phone, etc., and I eventually decided to take a chance and asked him if he wanted to come with me to Florida for the weekend. Even though we had never met each other in person, he agreed to go with me.

Sure enough, it turned out that he had just gotten out of prison for murder and drug dealing. I found this out on the airplane as we were winging our way towards Miami. *Great. No one knows that he's here in Florida with me, except maybe his parole officer.* I could tell that he didn't, um, get out much, because he brought a bath towel along with him, not knowing that they actually provide those for you at the hotel. We get to the hotel room and he promptly goes into the bathroom. He comes back out again, completely naked, holding a wide assortment of paraphernalia that he brought along that he thought gay guys would like. Then he tells me, "I can't force you to do anything, because that would be rape." My life was flashing before my eyes at this point. Everything turned out okay in the end, but he was kind of a pain in the ass. He was like a two year-old going away for the weekend for the first time. (Which was probably not far from the truth, actually.) I slept with one eye open the whole time for the rest of the weekend though. **„**

# Looking for a Few Good Friends

I am a 30 something black male living in Norfolk. I am just an
ordinary person. I am not cool, nor sophisticated, but I do
consider myself a nice and giving person. I am a faithful
friend that you can count on. I don't get out much only
because it is usually by myself and that's no fun. When I do
scrape up the courage to go out I enjoy traveling, movies,
festivals, concerts and theater. When I am at home I work out
about five days a week and go bicycle riding at the ocean-
front. When I am relaxing I unwind to the sounds of classical
jazz pieces. As I get older, being alone is getting, well...
you know how that can be. I am hoping through this medium I do
meet some special people who have the same sensibilities as I
do. I hope I find a person who is goal oriented, likes to have
fun, try new things and basically live life to the fullest.

" I have met people in the past via online dating, but as of late with this ad there has been only one response – but that was from someone in the Bahamas. I chose not reply to it only because we both would have lost interest in each other over time. I've encountered this numerous times in the past so this is no different. I did meet a really great guy several years ago online. He was absolutely perfect. He was a real gentleman and successful, intelligent, considerate and kind. I felt so comfortable with him. We went out a few times and would occasionally spend time at my apartment just watching TV. I really had a nice time with him but after a while he just left town and disappeared completely. I've never seen nor heard from him ever again. But to this day, I think about him often.

I guess I started using the Internet to meet people because I believed online dating would expose me to many more interesting people. I guess a more "traditional" method would be to meet people at the bars, but the bar scene is not something that I am really into. You never really meet any decent people there anyway.

While I'm not embarrassed about my placing or answering online ads, I also don't normally make it a point to discuss my online dating activities much either, only because it's really not so much of a big deal to me. Since online dating is fast becoming the most preferred way to meet people, those who use this method treat this as a normal dating ritual. So I don't feel the need to hide or broadcast the fact that I've been meeting people this way.

That said, I think that our society has changed a lot and I see this in the dating arena. We have become so obsessed with physical appearances and material possessions that we have totally forgotten to look at a person's heart.

And all the reality dating shows on television these days don't exactly help combat this. We choose to look for the material things to make us happy first and then (hopefully) the love will come later. I can tell you from personal experience that if you get involved with anyone for anything other than building a wholesome and loving relationship, you are asking for trouble. In the gay community, it's become all about SEX, SEX, SEX and more SEX. There are very little role models portraying committed relationships. Our very own culture perpetuates vanity and promiscuity. I unfortunately feel that things will only get worse. 99

# Lean, Lanky, and Willing

5"11, br/gr, 155, 39, wm. Lean, lanky, and smooth.
Nice smile, butt, and legs. Looking for a guy who's
passionate, relaxed, communicative, and into kissing, sucking,
j/o after a long day. Let's get in the shower together and
wash the day off and take it slow.
Evenings work well.


STD and HIV-. UB2. I can host.

" My first experience with this sort of thing occurred soon after I moved into my current apartment nine months ago. I had spent a considerable amount of time nesting: painting, buying furniture, and generally making my apartment my own. It was the first apartment that I'd lived alone in. Up until that point I'd had roommates and never the privacy to invite others to my personal space.

Perhaps I should say at the outset that I've always viewed the Men for Men listings as sex experiments. While in the back of my mind I am relationship minded, what I like about this particular forum is that it's free and that people here are here first for sex. This is different than going to a bar. People there might be with friends, for cocktails, blowing off some steam after work, but their intentions are not clear until after you've talked.

There's also the problem with introducing someone who might not be interested, the embarrassment that comes along with rejection when one is propositioned or propositions.

Here I'm free to send my face pic (always a face pic for me and never a body pic) to someone who fits my criteria whether or not they find me attractive. It's up to them to respond. And if they don't, well that's fine. At least I know.

I don't go for people who explicitly want risky sexual behavior such as bare backing, or swallowing. To that extent, I eschew role-playing scenarios and look for guys who suggest body contact, jacking off, sucking. Sure I've had safe anal sex on occasion, but I never respond to ads that list that as the primary motive. I sometimes ask guys if they like to kiss. This is a sort of barometer. I find that if a guy says, "No," then they're interested in a purely sex act, which is their prerogative, but I like intimacy as well.

My first two experiences (more or less nine months ago) occurred with two different guys. The first one didn't end up looking anything like his photo. He'd gained a lot of weight, was defensive and a bit jaded when I invited him over. We did get naked, but I ultimately asked him to leave in a diplomatic way. The next experience was with a nice guy around my age (I'm 40, he was 44). He had a nice build along with a nice personality. We had sex a couple of times but he was HIV+ and he wanted to fuck me from the start. He was prepared to do so with a condom but he also suggested that I fuck him without a condom. He pursued me for a while but I was turned off by his failure to build any sort of trust with me (I'm HIV-). After that I didn't go back online for five or six months.

In truth, online dating as opposed to finding sex online has never really appealed to me. There's too much interviewing and list checking, and for me takes out the spontaneity of meeting someone in person (though I did date someone briefly that I met on a gay dating site who is now a friend). I used to like going out to bars and meeting guys. But after a few years that has lost its appeal. I don't enjoy the alcohol that surrounds such meetings.

I definitely find myself changing my views as I grow older. I was married in my twenties and have a daughter, and I've since found that as I grow older, I'm freer with my sexuality and I don't attach such emotion to it. It's a need to be fulfilled and I see each meeting as such. What's interesting to me is that when I think about a good relationship, I'd rather meet someone through a hobby or activity I have interest in. People always ask how you've met someone you're dating and ultimately I'd probably not like to admit that I met someone online for sex and it went from there!

With that said, in the last month I've tried the personals again five or six times – all of which were successful and fulfilling. I've had sex with a black guy, an asian, and three or four white guys. Most have been in their thirties or early forties, but two were in their late twenties. This surprised me because I've normally been attracted to guys around my age. Out of the six or so sexual experiences I've had, none were repeat performances. I have been in contact with the asian guy by email, but nothing has transpired. What I've found about meeting people (men) this way is that most aren't looking to find a boyfriend through these experiences, and neither am I. Sure, the potential is there, but I don't put such expectations on it. I'd rather just enjoy the moment and avoid any undue pressure.

Interestingly enough only one person has held my attention —
a guy I didn't end up having sex with. He placed an ad, I
responded, we flirted, and then ended up e-mailing for four or
five days and talking on the phone. Although he was very attractive, he was also sensitive, playful, communicative, revealing.
What was interesting is that he initially said in our early conversations that he'd seen my profile on a couple of dating sites
last fall (I had these up for maybe a month) and that he saw
something unique in my photo and profile. So when I sent him
my photo, he later expressed that meeting me felt like destiny.
That was pretty exciting for me when he turned out to be much
more attractive in person. He'd also been married in his twenties
and has two children so this also interested me. We had a common bond.

We met briefly for coffee and had a nice kiss on a corner near
where both of us live. But then a few days later he cancelled a
lunch date.

Looking back, I expressed too much interest in him in our
emails, I was perhaps too forward, and I think that intensity
put him off. Would I change that? I'm not sure. But it was good
mirroring of what two people go through when they meet online
or off. He said that it felt a bit intense between us and I apolo-
gized and backed off. I haven't contacted him, but he's sent me
an email saying that he hasn't forgotten about me at all and
that he'll contact me soon once things settle down. I don't know
if he ever will. But he has dominated my thoughts because our

interaction was different and I felt something for him, however early in the process that might have been.

The funny thing is, I could have met him anywhere and the outcome would have probably been the same – we just happened to meet online. **,,**

# Something more than sex...

Posting this one more time.

19m here. 6'0 dirty blond, blue eyes, 165, vgl.

Looking for something more than a one-time thing. Like very masculine guys who are mature, intelligent, and good looking :-).

20-30 is good, but age is less important than personality. If you're good looking, masculine, looking for something a little more than a one time hook-up, whether it be friends with benefits, or a boyfriend, shoot me your info and a picture. I realize that this is a long shot but thought there was a fighting chance that there was a little more than extremely horny flamboyant guys on here.

" Upon the roughly 15-20 responses to my ad post, I wrote back to 5 or 6 asking for a follow-up and a new list of questions. After this "second screening" I started speaking with only one guy via email. We met up, made some sort of connection, had a good time, and that was that. I have his email but now the intrigue is missing. The reason being . . . well I'm not quite sure. The Internet is a very peculiar place, allowing for many of us to dream and fantasize out loud. I can post asking for Eden and can easily expect that I will get it back. The problem always happens when it leaves the Internet. This is when fantasy becomes reality and no fantasy can be real. In a way it's an emotional outlet that allows people to connect mentally in an electronic world, but leaves no consideration for the physical reality that exists. Long story short, I guess I will keep participating in the electronic union. It's always fun to dream. "

# masc. man seeks quality NOT quantity...................

I'm not into any lifestyle. I just happen to be attracted to other men.

48, 6'1", 220, hairy, brown/blue, good-looking, very masculine. Like the outdoors, ocean, hiking, biking, camping. No bs here. Looking to meet another very masculine guy who DOESN'T go to bars and who DOESN'T think it strange that I haven't been with a guy in a long time......... preferably my age or younger, any color, culture, race religion, blah blah blah.................

Oh yeah, and someone with balls enough to work at something.

"I've never met anyone online and I haven't met anyone otherwise for quite some time. My one and only relationship lasted five years, and ended six years ago. I'm not looking for instant gratification so it's been hard to meet people of any substance who aren't just after a quick/easy screw.

Men are controlled by their sexual needs and always want it right now – they lose interest if you don't meet them right away. And gay men have no barriers. I'm not interested in anyone who sleeps around, which is very hard to find in a gay man.

Most men I've encountered online aren't interested in e-mailing or talking and getting to know a person before they have sex. They lose interest quickly like little boys.

I'm looking for quality, not quantity, and it's sadly

proving to be elusive. I'm also not into the gay scene or lifestyle, which is something else most gay men can't seem to comprehend.

It's been hard to meet another guy strong enough to stand alone and who doesn't need the "safety in numbers" mentality of the gay world. If you're not into the gay "lifestyle" and don't consider yourself "gay" (homo not gay – gay is a lifestyle, not a sexual orientation) then you're not accepted.

I refuse to allow myself to be labeled and categorized. Who I love or have sex with has zero to do with my personality or lifestyle, and I won't be ghettoized. The gay world has become highly judgmental over the years, which is a shame because when I "came out" in the seventies it was just the opposite; gay people were the most accepting and open people.

I return to school at the age of 53 in September and hope to meet someone there. Once in a while I'll keep trying the Net but I have few expectations of meeting anyone of quality there. It's scary that after all the deaths from AIDS that so few have learned their lessons. **99**

# Not A Word

My house.
You rap on the window.
I open the door.
My bedroom.
Your pants fall.
I suck you.
You come.
You leave.
Not a word is spoken.

" I'm a sex addict. A slut. A whore. I admit it. I've slept with at least five men who are married to women. I've blown a man in his garage while his partner was asleep. I jerked off with a gay man while watching straight gangbang porn. I kicked back and let a man suck me off while smoking cigarettes and blowing the smoke in his face. A week later, I would suck him while his boyfriend took me from behind. I've been verbally instructed to give someone a tongue bath and I've been verbally assaulted in a humiliation scene (my least favorite, but at least now I know what it feels like). I've fisted a stranger and tied up a few near-strangers. I've slept with a boy of 19 and a man of 58 (and everything in between). On my 45th birthday, I put out a post for someone to come over and strip down and give me a show. The gentleman who responded was incredibly sexy and we've seen each other twice since. I've posted ads for outdoor anonymous sex and been lucky enough to find a few other like-minded individuals who'd willingly drop trout in our city's most adorable public parks. One night, I had the urge to sleep with a large man (meaning "fat"), but the respondent thought I meant large penis. No complaints once the game began, as he was slightly pudgy but with the largest dick I've seen in a good while. Only because this is a confidential and private account of my online trysts will I report that I've let three men do to me what really, really, really gets me hard: erotic asphyxiation.

This, however, was the most successful post I've created and my favorite scene to date. I truly felt the need to reduce sex to its most primal nature: mere grunts and hand motions. While in my bedroom, with my roommate next door asleep, a knock came at the window. I opened the door, let a tall stranger enter the room, turned off the lights, disrobed him, sucked him off, dressed him back up and sent him on his way. He was a physical type that normally doesn't interest me (wiry and compact). Yet, it was most thrilling. Who he was, where he came from, why he wanted to join me in this, I will never know. I was reduced to an animal, as was he, and none were the wiser.

Looking back, I realize why it was so successful for me. I got to the core of my homosexuality. Stripping away the nonsense of bars, the alcohol, the cover charge, the taking-a-shower-before-you-go, the flattering lighting, the banal chit-chat, the mating ritual of trying to size-up the men around the room, the dreadful music, the social constructs of "gay culture." There were no irritations or obstacles. In this simple ad post, I pared away all frivolity and got exactly what I wanted from another man at that moment. **"**

# "COULD BE AN INTERESTING TRYST"

MISSED CONNECTIONS

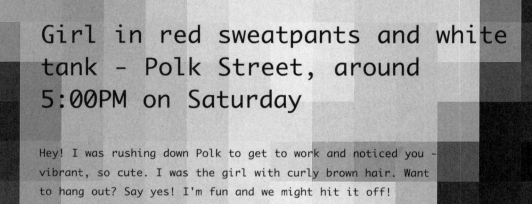

Girl in red sweatpants and white tank - Polk Street, around 5:00PM on Saturday

Hey! I was rushing down Polk to get to work and noticed you - vibrant, so cute. I was the girl with curly brown hair. Want to hang out? Say yes! I'm fun and we might hit it off!

" The Missed Connections ads hold a certain mystique for me. It's where the most interesting fantasies converge in the personals section of the paper, or in this case, online. These are not the vague desires to meet an abstract someone; these hopes are pinned to a certain smile, a certain gaze, a certain walk, a certain bus ride, a certain foggy night, a specific moment of loneliness and yearning and hope for possibility. I believe people who write in Missed Connections are often the true hopeless romantics in the personals world. This is not a pragmatic attempt at meeting a mate. A Missed Connection ad comes directly from the obscure, needy subconscious that has latched onto a spontaneous, exciting and ambiguous enough interaction to engender all types of wondering for the imaginative mind. I think that, usually, the person who is writing the Missed Connection ad is writing up the ad from pure dream stuff. And then there's a sense of destiny; if she sees this posting, then it was meant to be, even if it doesn't last.

I have posted a few Missed Connections ads now. The first one I can remember is from Gay Pride weekend just last month. Already Gay Pride was loaded for me this year again – I knew I'd be seeing hundreds of beautiful girls and I hoped I would meet one of them, but didn't believe I ever would. Also there would be lots of ecstatic, cute couples there. I went to the Girls' Short Film Program at the Castro Theatre and was amazed by the sheer quantity of cute, smart looking women in one place. A part of me immediately became sad as I thought, "Why can't I ever meet one of these girls? And today will not be an exception." I don't mean to be self-defeatist, but I just had the feeling I would see and wonder, but I would not have the opportunity to actually talk to anyone.

Seated ahead of me and my friends with her friends was a cute tan woman about my age, 30ish with neck-length, light brown hair kissed by the sun and serious eyes. I made eye contact with her and smiled. She smiled back. Our eyes met a couple more times before the show.

I never had the opportunity to talk to her. I didn't notice her leave after the show as my friends and I launched excitedly into an analysis of the films we had just seen. I placed an ad on the Missed Connections forum because I just thought, "Well, what if she thought I was cute too, and is as curious as me to meet someone new?"

I never heard from her. That was several years ago. In July, I posted another ad. I was having a great day. I had finished helping a friend move and I was zipping down Polk Street in the fading warm weather. I passed a pretty, young woman in her twenties.

She was wearing bright red sweatpants and a flattering white "wife-beater" tank top. Honestly, she looked hot! She had long, clean dark brown hair, beautiful brown skin from an ethnic background I could not determine (Filipina I guessed). We walked by each other, and I looked at her in passing. She shot me a vibrant smile. Her eyes lit up. I smiled back, quite elated. I thought, "Wow what a nice, beautiful girl!" But, how do you meet someone when you are rushing down the street to work? (And I was running late.) It was just a smile after all. Later, I thought about her while I was at work, distracted, all day long.

I could see her beautiful smile in my mind. I started with the same thoughts I always get about random beautiful smiles and somewhat lingering eye contact. What if she had smiled at me because she thought I was cute? What if she wants to meet a nice girl, too? What if she saw in me what I saw in her – spontaneity, strength, beauty, charm and energy? I posted my ad but I never heard anything from her. She was not looking for me.

Last year I did meet a woman online though. I responded to her Women Seeking Women ad, which caught my eye because she wanted to meet a relatively "normal" woman. I happened to read her ad in a moment when I was feeling disenchanted with the plethora of girls that have an extremely tomboyish look that I am not into.

Of course, we did not hit it off. She was a boring lawyer and I realized proudly that I am not normal! ”

# Seeking Flight Attendant

Four days ago on a flight from Hong Kong to San Francisco, a beautiful flight attendant put a note on my snack tray that said, "I want you," the last snack before we landed. She also pressed her butt against my shoulder several times (I was in an aisle seat). So I was flattered, since there were a lot of guys there, and was glad that she obviously liked Asian guys. Anyway, she wore a striking ring on her right middle finger, was about 5'4" tall, slim and the most-friendly Flight Attendant there, even though the others were kewl too. But if you see this, holla. . . your email doesn't work, or it's overloaded. Or, if one of your friends see this, holla . . . and I'll take you all to dinner in Hong Kong or San Francisco. Yeah, she had the sexy vibe, all the guys noticed her, even over the other Flight Attendants who were all pretty to beautiful too.

" She sent me an email about a week ago in response to this posting, and we'll meet probably in San Francisco in a few weeks. I will also be in Hong Kong anyway the end of this month, so I can also take her and her friend to dinner, as I promised in my ad. It's likely the friend is cute too, so I may introduce her to a friend of mine in Hong Kong.

She said that she was really very shocked to hear from me, but that it was a nice shock. She thought I threw her note away or something. She wasn't so much shocked to have heard from me because she had given me her email address and expected me to contact her. She was more 'shocked' because of the way I actually got in touch with her and how it all turned out – that I had to go through this Missed Connections forum to reach her. (I had originally tried to contact her through the email address she gave me, but her mail bin was full or something, so I couldn't get through.)

There were about a half dozen flight attendants on that flight, and most of them were very pretty, which is unusual because typically there may be just one or two hot ones. I noticed that guys on the plane were certainly checking them out and enjoying themselves! I guess we were all lucky on this flight to have so many of them there together. Anyway, she was the most beautiful one on board that day. She had a face like an angel, medium length brown hair, kissable lips and eyes, slim face with a slim body, and great legs. In Hong Kong, there are always a lot of pretty girls walking around in the streets, and some of them look better than movie stars. She is one of those. I was attracted to her not only for her physical looks, but she was also the friendliest one there with the nicest smile and manner. She was nice to everyone. Of course, Flight Attendants should be like that, but she was a cut above. That said, I do have to say that she was also very, very sexy. And she kept pressing her butt against my shoulder. Once could be an accident, but not several times. Even the older guy beside me was noticing it, I think. There's plenty of space on the aisle not to bump a shoulder, if you don't need to. After this happened a couple of times, I decided that I was going to approach her, but she beat me to it by slipping me the note.

This is the first time I've searched for someone like this. I just learned about all this and the Missed Connections postings a few weeks ago from a writer friend of mine. Coincidence, I guess. I also believe in synchronicity. When one believes the world is amazing, amazing things tend to happen. 99

# Girl who is killing me at Calif. and Leavenworth

Who would have thought 8:30 am would become my favorite time of day? I'm always anticipating you being on the corner on my walk to work, your smile makes my day. Where can I find you after hours?

" I haven't met this particular person yet, but I have met, and do continue to meet, people online. I even had a one-year relationship with a girl in Colombia, which was, in a word, *intense*.

I speak fluent Spanish, which I think was part of her initial attraction to me when we first met on the Internet. Over time, we wrote to each other constantly through email. We exchanged photos and I grew more and more attracted to her every day. She was super-cute, witty and very intelligent. We exchanged phone numbers and our emails turned into phone calls, so we were able to connect our voices with our photos and written words and we spoke frequently. Finally, after about five months, I decided to take the risk and planned a trip to go over there to see her.

While Columbia isn't the safest place for an American to travel to during the best of times, I had to go see her and I couldn't contain my curiosity any longer.

So I went to meet her with high hopes, but tried to limit our expectations in case things didn't work out or we didn't click the same way in person. We both agreed that upon meeting each other in person, if we didn't feel the same attraction immediately that we had experienced online, we'd go our separate ways and have no hard feelings. I didn't want any undo pressure on either of us and just wanted to experience things naturally.

Well, we hit it off immediately and we had a wonderful time together – it was a fantastic week! We fell in love and I hated to go back to the States. When I returned home, we resumed our telephone and email chats and things were going great (as great as they could be for a long distance romance anyway). This went on for several months and I began planning for my next trip to go visit her again in South America. It was during this trip when she started showing me her true colors.

Maybe I was being naive, but while my first trip over there had absolutely no expectations, the second trip was completely full of them. While she never actually said it, I think she was expecting me to propose to her on this trip.

Perhaps it was because of the distance, and the overall intensity of our relationship, but there was growing pressure to accelerate things since we didn't know when we'd actually see each other again. But I just can't move that fast when it comes to something like marriage.

A week into this second trip she grew more and more demanding and started to excel at finding new ways of getting into my wallet. I found myself buying her and her family and friends all kinds of expensive gifts. We'd be strolling down the street and she'd spy a dress or shoes or something in the window and would persuade me to buy them for her. This happened all the time. Before I even flew over there, she said that she had a friend who was having a baby and asked if I could buy something for them and bring it over with me. (I've never even met these people.) I even bought her a nice stereo system that was far better than the one I had in my own home.

Don't get me wrong, as I am actually a very generous and giving person. But there are limits to my wealth and this was quickly becoming more of an "expected" part of our relationship and a side of her personality that I hadn't witnessed before.

And then I saw another side of her that I also wasn't expecting. It happened at the hotel where I was staying. She had a heated altercation with the hotel manager about the rate I was being charged for my room. Within two minutes she became unruly and they had threatened to call the police. Being in a country that wasn't completely safe for Americans traveling, the last thing I wanted was any extra attention or, worse yet, have any run-ins with the local police. That was a big warning bell right there as I witnessed the intensity and fury that she was capable of exhibiting towards a complete stranger. Little did I know that soon it would be turned towards me.

After I returned home I did some soul searching and decided that the best thing to do would be to start pulling away from her, thinking that the distance between us would be a barrier and that she'd find someone else. I think she must have gotten the hint because the next thing I knew, she was calling me thirty times a day at home and at the office making accusations, calling me names and threatening to blackmail me. She accused me of being unfaithful and having affairs because I often wasn't home when she'd call. I actually have a rather demanding job, which can often require me to work late and burn the midnight oil. She said that I was using her just to have this wild Latin-type affair and that I never really loved her. She twisted every good thing that I had ever done for her and said that they were all just excuses to get her to sleep with me. Then she told me that she was having health issues because of all this and resulting bills that she expected me to pay. It got to be so bad that in the end, I eventually had to disconnect my phone.

This all happened about two years ago. Since that time I've met other women online thinking that the worst experiences were now behind me. And then I met Sandra (not her real name) through an Internet dating site. She was a very attractive thirty-something divorcee and we hit it off almost immediately. We had gone out about three or four times together when she invited me over to her house one evening for dinner. Things were going great that night . . . until her "ex-husband" showed up. It turned out that she wasn't actually divorced after all – just recently separated. *Very* recently separated!

So he's not at all happy to see me there, and flies into a rage. He's running around the outside of the house trying to force entry inside, while she's trying her best to keep him out by making sure all points of entry were secure. I needed her to phone the police since I couldn't remember the address and couldn't really describe where I was, but she wouldn't. She kept saying that he was "nice" and that he wouldn't do anything, etc. Eventually he gave up and went away and she said, "See? I told you everything would be all right."

Sure enough, shortly afterwards he turned up again and tried to force his way in once more. This time, she did call the police but he left before they could arrive. I left not too long after that.

As I was driving away, I noticed a car following behind me. I assured myself that I was just being paranoid and that it couldn't actually be him, but of course it was. The idiot followed me for several blocks but eventually gave up, lost interest or who knows what made him decide to stop.

It's enough to make you think twice about using the Internet to meet and date people. I have heard a lot of success stories from other people though, so perhaps there's hope.

I've found that this is the only real viable outlet to meet people here in San Francisco. I've used it to initiate a lot of first dates over the last year and a half since I moved here, but not a lot of second ones. ""

# To the police officer on    the horse who sent me to   jail last night.

I was the one who slapped your horse on the ass and called him Buttercup. My friends were dying. Cute girls even laughed. I guess you didn't like that too much. I was a little drunk.

-Nicholas

" The cop yelled at me, and I began to run off, but I was drunk and not getting too far in any one direction. And my friends didn't run at all, so I thought it was pretty fruitless and gave up. He held me until the paddy-wagon came, which was full of a bunch of other drunks. Eight of us spent the night in two cells, and we got a little snack before we went to bed, so it wasn't all bad. I don't know why I did it, but it sure seemed funny at the time. My friends couldn't believe it and were all cracking up. So were the people around at the time, including some very cute girls, which I think just made the cop even more pissed off. I actually ended up hooking up with one of the girls during the power outage later in the summer. She didn't know it was me until the next morning, when we were telling stories. I wouldn't repeat the experience again, but I'm glad to have had the experience – I love that kind of stuff. "

# A year later and I still think of you!

It's been almost a year since I last saw you. You probably hate me for just dropping all communication, but I had to for reasons that weren't directly related to you. But the problem is I still think about you a lot. When we got together, I had no idea that you would impact me the way you did. Honestly, my feelings for you were really strong. I know it's too late now, for all I know you have a boyfriend now or maybe you even moved. But know at least this - I will never forget you, and I will always be sad for what might have been if I hadn't been so scared to take a chance....

" I never heard from my Missed Connection. And to tell the truth, I think the odds are pretty slim. I've learned from reading the various Missed Connections postings, that people are just afraid — afraid of opening up, afraid of rejection, and afraid of themselves. I wish that I had heard from her. I have been in a relationship that hasn't always been great. But there has been one person, my Missed Connection, that made me feel like fireworks were going off in my head when we kissed. I have since given up on this true love crap. "

# Seeking Sister of a Girl "Morning Dew" I met from Newark to Dallas

I'm from Denver and met a girl at Newark Airport a few years ago. She was flying to Dallas to meet her sister. I helped this girl at the terminal in Newark get to the right gate, etc. The girl I met was Jewish and her name translated meant "morning dew". She was a model and maybe her sister was too. Drop me a line.

66 Making that connection happen was a shot in the dark.

I met this beautiful Jewish girl from Israel at Newark Airport in August of 2000. I was checking in for my flight when I noticed her. She was very confused about her travel, so I assisted her. She was actually at the wrong airport. Go figure. Her flight was out of JFK. The airline accommodated her anyway.

So I spent the next hour or so talking with her. All I know is that she was visiting her sister in Dallas who might be a model, her dad was a Rabbi, and she was staying in New York.

Unfortunately, she was on a later flight. I tried to get her on my flight to Dallas but they told me it was booked.

We had an amazing connection. So much that I was at the wrong gate just sitting with her and falling for her amazing beauty when they paged my name over the PA. The plane was waiting for me to get on. I had no idea that I was late. Talk about getting caught up in the moment!

I gave her my number of my cell phone in Denver and we just stared at each other before embracing and exchanging small kisses on the cheek.

I finally got on the plane, only to discover to my horror that there was an open seat right next to me! I wanted to go running back after her, but of course at this point it was too late.

Eventually I arrived in Dallas, and would have gladly waited for her flight to come in, but I would have missed the connection to Denver, which was really ironic, and couldn't afford to do.

The next day I went up to Mount Evans for a drive. At 14,000 feet cell phones have no chance. When I finally descended, I had a message from her that was all garbled. I guess she tried to call me but failed to connect. I never heard from her again. **"**

## PGB

How nice life would be if I hadn't ruined things between us.
I should have waited until my issues were resolved and I was
healed before pursuing you. But that's not how it happened.
And for the rest of my life I will live with the guilt and
shame of causing you pain. I hope that you are happy and at
peace. I think of you often, and always wish the best for you.

" PGB and I met at work several years ago. I was married and pregnant at the time. I had no intentions or desire to fall in love with someone else, but fate had a different plan . . . or so it seemed. After I gave birth to my daughter, I began to realize how infatuated I was with PGB. I dreamt about him almost every night, but these were very particular dreams, where I felt connected to him spiritually. I was almost sure that he felt it too. It took a while for me to approach him with my feelings, but once I did, I knew for certain that he felt for me in a similar manner. He didn't want to do anything to come between my husband and myself, so he kept his distance.

I was writing in my journal about my feelings for PGB. I truly believed that this person was my soul mate. I had never felt a connection or attraction to another person so strong in my life.

My then-husband found the journal, and a drama began. He threatened him and gave me a decent amount of grief as well, to put it lightly. In all actuality, PGB had done nothing. I was guilty only of being in love with another man. PGB quit his job and found other employment in the region.

After a time, we happened to come in contact with one another again. We had mutual friends and still worked in the same industry. After approximately two years of trying to "fix" what was wrong in the marriage and "sticking it out for the kids" I realized I was dying a slow and miserable death. I decided to leave. About this same time, PGB and I became romantically involved.

Leaving my husband was very difficult. To avoid the nasty fight which I was sure would ensue, I opted to leave my two children with him. My leaving was going to be hard enough; there didn't need to be a custody battle in the middle of it. Knowing how my then-husband felt about PGB, I did everything I could to keep him from finding out that I was involved with him. I knew that he would assume that I had left him for PGB. This sounds maybe a bit flaky, but I didn't want him to know for fear of what he might do to PGB or myself.

While trying to keep my then-husband from finding out, I managed to destroy the one thing that I believed so deeply in. At the time, I was trying to get out of the relationship gently. I feared my ex-husband's anger. There were a lot of concessions made at the time, which were made out of fear, out of a need to keep him from blowing up. I found myself sleeping with the then-husband on a couple of different occasions, thinking that he wouldn't suspect another man if I gave in to his requests for sex. Looking back, it was the stupidest thing I have ever done in my life. I can't believe how ignorant and manipulative I was.

PGB found out about what had been going on and things became very difficult in that relationship. There was a lot of anger, a lot of yelling. I knew that he had some issues with trust, and instead of trying to help him overcome them, I ended up justifying his lack of trust. I became depressed pretty quickly, and completely overwhelmed by the drama that I had managed to bring into my life. I asked PGB for some time apart. I only wanted six months. He took it that I was breaking up with him. After the six months had passed, I tried on several occasions to get back together with him, to explain to him my regret, my shame for my behavior. But PGB doesn't believe in the words "I'm sorry" and my words fell short.

Unfortunately, there is no hope for absolution or forgiveness. I will always live with the regret of losing the one man who I believed to be my soul mate, and I will always be ashamed of my behavior. I have learned some very hard lessons from the whole experience.

My attempt to reach out to PGB is purely selfish. I discovered that I needed to forgive myself. The last contact I had with him netted me a nasty response; very cruel, acidic and mean. I can't say that I blame him. I know that PGB no longer lives in the area, having moved to Atlanta. I could contact him directly if I wanted to, but I don't really want to. I am assuming that he has moved on with his life and I hope with all my heart that he has found peace, happiness, and someone who can show him that not all women are screwed up. But, I needed to make some kind of a gesture, for myself. I had this need, this feeling that I had to do something to assure myself that I had tried to earnestly, honestly and deeply apologize. "

# Beautiful Boy

You were on the train from Surbiton to Wimbledon this morning.
It made my day when you smiled back at me.  I'm sorry I was
too shy to talk to you.

" As it happens I met my Missed Connection yesterday on the train and he's even more beautiful than I remembered. He is the type of person you look at and have to catch your breath because he looks so intense. I am not usually shy, but he caught me in a timid bubble. He introduced himself after we saw each other again on the platform. I didn't think I'd ever see him again and couldn't help blushing when he came over. We talked about sweet-nothings, fare dodged and bought white Lilies. They were for his girlfriend I think. It's already a romantic tragedy.

It turned out he went to school with my friend's brothers . . . small world. I didn't think he would ever see the M/C posting, but I wanted to post it as a small expression of how a briefly intimate moment (a smile) can make you happy and curious for the rest of the day. "

# Saw you in the laundry room

We were both downstairs doing laundry-
You: the wash
Me: getting my stuff out of the dryer.
You are so cute, but unfortunately, I was too shy to say
anything to you on the elevator so we both rode up to the
4th floor in awkward silence. Wish I had said something.....

66 This was a post about an interesting guy I saw one day in my building. Aside from finding him attractive, I found he had a quiet demeanor I was drawn to, and when we rode the elevator up to the fourth floor, and we both got out, I noticed that he looked as if he was going to say something, and then decided not to. When I got back up to my apartment, I decided to post this Missed Connection online. Unfortunately, nothing came of it. Not that I really expected it to, or that I would even know how to react had he actually read it and responded! I did have this little fantasy in my mind that he would respond, and a torrid romance would begin. Rich fantasy life! Seen too many movies I guess. What I find amusing about the whole Missed Connections phenomenon, especially in my case, is that I could've just said something to him, and since we're in the same building, tracked him down. Of course, doing that would just mean

facing immediate approval or rejection, and I think that's why there are so many posts. We are prolonging a romanticized notion of what we think could be an interesting tryst. Perhaps that's just me. I think the anonymity of it all makes it that much more exciting, knowing that maybe, just maybe, the person you saw on the subway across from you, or the crush you have at work, or the guy in the laundry room, could be thinking the same thing and might actually read what you wrote and write back.

I actually met my ex boyfriend online in 2000. When I first got a computer early that year, my roommate and I decided, on a dare to each other, to put ads up on Planet Out. I actually ended up meeting some cool people through it, although there were a few who didn't even match their picture! Anyway, I was on AIM one night chatting with friends, and someone popped up on my screen. After chatting for a few hours, we exchanged numbers and agreed to meet. From that point we were together for two and a half years (we just broke up this summer). In retrospect, I don't think we would've given each other the time of day had we been in the same bar, or other public spot, as our personalities are vastly different. When you meet someone online, it's much easier to be vulnerable and honest than when you are face to face. The irony is, now he's met someone else online, also through a personal ad, and I'm watching a pattern repeat itself – and it's kind of sickening, to be honest. Basically, I think there is obviously something compelling about all this, perhaps just because it supplies us with a feeling of mystery. But I do think that it's making us a lot less capable of interacting with each other directly, as so many of us have become accustomed to doing everything through email and instant messaging. 99

# Fox & Hound girl / Kahala

You:
Waitress last night, wearing green shirt, out of soybeans, super nice, the most beautiful girl I have ever seen. When you got off duty at around 9:30pm my heart sank with the thought of never seeing you again.

Me:
Sitting at front booth, wearing brown, sharing ESB pitcher with friends, totally mesmerized by your charm & hospitality, hoping our paths will cross.

" My Missed Connections ad is totally legit & unfortunately I have received no response from the girl I am seeking. It may sound cheesy, but I was having some beers with my shipmates on vacation (I work on a cruise ship in the Caribbean), and there she was. The most beautiful girl I have ever seen in my entire life, our waitress, super hot and wicked cool, a total Drew Barrymore with dark hair = my dream woman. Her sincerity, her smile, her mannerisms were orgasmic.

After living in Waikiki and on international ships, I am exposed to raw beauty in heavy dosages. But nobody in my twenty-seven years has ever come close to the bar waitress at Ye Olde Fox & Hound pub near Kahala Mall that one lucky evening.

I was in shock, sweating profusely, and too scared

and/or shy to express any interest before she got off duty and vanished forever. I did manage to throw down a 125% gratuity on the pitcher bill. Living on a ship (three months on, one month off) doesn't necessarily help my land-based female companionship opportunities. But I swear my heart was racing and I would do anything in the world to see and/or speak to this girl again.

Of course, she probably never even saw my posting. My local friends made fun of me when they heard the story. Honolulu is still a little new to the online ads scene. But I just wished that maybe one of her friends or workmates would have seen the post and given her the heads-up. Oh well.

Believe it or not, deep down inside I have a feeling that someday, somewhere, I will see her again. Hopefully she won't be married because I want her to be my future wife. This probably sounds nuts but I'll never forget her and I fantasize about the day that she'll be mine. "

# five saturday night

I was sitting at the chair in the dance floor and could not keep myself from admiring you . . . contact me if you're interested. I would have asked you to dance, but I'd been out since 5pm and lacked enthusiasm to dance at 3am . . . For you I should have done it anyway though. Coffee?

66 I received two replies to my ad . . . one was from someone asking for more information and the second was from the person I was actually looking for. We met for a drink and I was completely bored out of my mind. We were better in my imagination than in real life. She was hot and a great dancer, but I didn't approach her initially because it wasn't clear to me if she had a boyfriend (she was dancing occasionally with the same guy a few times that night . . . turns out it was a friend). This M/C post was a neutral (shot in the dark) way of seeing if she was interested and available.

I think we were mutually attracted to each other but she and I clearly had little in common, unfortunately. She's a school counselor from Idaho and I'm a negotiator from New York. She's a great girl, don't get me wrong, but we just didn't click.

It took about five minutes to figure this out and an hour and a half to finally end the date. I'm sure she felt the same about me. At the end of the date we shook hands and didn't tell each other we'd call or see each other. We ended with a, "Hey, it was great to meet you. Good luck!" I immediately went out to join my friends at Spank afterwards.

I discovered the Missed Connections forum by accident a few months ago when a buddy told me a girl had posted an ad about me (he and I were out together and she described me and the venue perfectly). I met the girl and we dated a few times. We had lots of fun but we didn't make a "love" connection or anything. Honestly, it was really flattering to have someone post an M/C about me. Since then I've checked out the ads religiously about one to two times a week, but after this last experience I think I'll probably stop. I've tried Internet dating but have had disappointing results.

Everyone's profile is equally edgy, and hip, blah, blah, blah, but in real life they're not very interesting when you meet them. A forum like the Missed Connections ads is better than online dating though, because it's more visceral and directed to a particular person and situation. So as a result, it's more compelling but it's also completely random. I've learned it's more fun and easy to meet people in real life. So in a way, for me, online M/Cs and dating have made my real life experiences much better. ,,

# Hot yoga and a cold shower

We spoke in yoga this morning about taking a cold shower and I can't stop thinking about you. You are one of the sexiest guys I have seen in a long time. Just wanted the cosmos to know I am sitting at my desk trying to complete a form about something I can't understand because you have taken control of my mind.

" This Missed Connection posting was a result of my morning yoga class. I wasn't expecting any response from it. It was really more of a way to process what happened to me earlier. I oftentimes use email and the Internet as my psychiatrist.

There was a guy in class who was visiting from another city (I think). He was about 6'3", curly red hair, and in the words of Daisy, hulking. Very sexy for me. We spoke for a few minutes in the locker room after class. He said he made it through class thinking about taking a cold shower afterward and asked if my shower was cold enough when I was done. Like many casual meetings in life, we connected for a few minutes in a real way, and went on with our routines. I knew I'd never see him again. However, I was having trouble concentrating at work because I kept thinking about this guy. So to clear my head, I posted my appreciation for him online. My thought was released into the cosmos and I was able to return to the task at hand. (It was that or go jack off in the men's room.)

I do occasionally use online forums in just this fashion. I love posting and reading the personals, especially the Rants and Raves and the Missed Connections on Craigslist and Backpage.com. The ability to speak one's mind is so cathartic, and I use these tools with the understanding that the message will not get to the intended party, but that's okay. It is no longer my responsibility – it is with the higher powers.

I use email in the same fashion. I often type long emails responding to people as a way to process my thoughts, and when I'm done I just hit the 'delete' button. Last week though, I actually hit 'send' instead of 'delete' (oops) which resulted in a pretty funny exchange.

I also use email to meet people. I am disciplined by a dominator that I met online, and he and I spend a lot of time working each other up electronically before our meetings. But that, as they say, is a whole other story. 99

# Man with ear boo boo - w4m

My missed connection is a white guy, 30's, brown hair, with a
mangled left ear.
I was on a flight to Oakland on Saturday with him.
I thought he was yummy.
Someone must know him.

"The funny thing is that someone did reply to my ad that was on my flight and he had injured his ear and was wearing a band-aid on it, during the flight. He was not the person I was looking for. I was looking for a man whose ear was so severely damaged, it was pretty much missing, with a significant amount of scar tissue. He was sitting in the waiting area across from me before boarding and he kept staring at me. I found him quite attractive and did not see his ear. I was following him onto the plane with the intention of sitting next to him, but we got separated when his carry on was too large for the overhead bin. The man who responded to my posting was certain he was the man I was looking for. He wanted to meet me and he was young and attractive. (An opera singer no less.) But I'm not going to. I'm still looking for my handsome earless fellow."

# You have a new dog....

I see you walking your dog along the Ave. I've seen you for
several years. You no longer have your black lab and you now
have a bulldog. I've seen your hair grey a bit. Don't know if
you're married or single?
I've longed to speak to you.

66 I've met hundreds of people off the Internet and have made a few lifelong friends as a result. But so far, I haven't met anyone romantically yet. In this particular instance, I live in the area and any shyness that I might be feeling aside, I don't feel that it's appropriate for me to be yelling anything from my car window while driving by when I see him. I have made eye contact with him though and my daughter teases me all of the time when she arrives home and has seen "my guy" out. It's gotten to be a bit of a household joke. I just figured, "What the heck? There might be a chance that he reads these things."

Maybe this is what encouraged me to do this. I visited my son in Portland a couple of weeks ago, and just before I arrived there, my son (who plays in a local rock band) had met this girl after their set. He visited with her for almost two hours in the bar and knew that her name was Theresa. The time got away from him and she eventually said, "It's late. I gotta get going." So she left and he stood there in the bar kicking himself because he didn't get her number. He later asked the bartender if she frequented the place. He told him that he'd seen her there a few times, but mostly on Friday nights. So needless to say, my son went there the next Friday night, stayed all night waiting for her, and of course, no Theresa. Apparently they have a free newspaper in Portland and inside there is a section called; *I Saw You*. My son posted a note there saying, "THERESA – I met you in the bar after my band played, we talked, it got late you had to leave. I DIDN'T get your number. Please email me," and included his email address.

The paper was on the newsstand for just a few hours when he received an email that said, "I don't normally play on computers and I don't remember your name. Call me and re-introduce yourself." So he did! Turns out she lives only two blocks from him and they are now dating and getting to know one another.

So you never know! These personals do really work sometimes. I just might actually meet my man with the new dog one day. I guess time will tell. "

# I have a budgie in my bathroom

Did you lose him/her? I would love to give it back to the
owner as I have two cats and I don't think a trio would work
out. Please email and describe, and even  better - email a
photo.

" I'll start with the budgie. I posted in various places on Craigslist about the bird since I was hoping that someone in my neighborhood would know about it, or even own it. I've had much success in the past with postings for various needs/reasons and thought that someone would at least contact me with advice, owner information, or a cage. I ended up receiving replies for each one but the owner. Personally, I think that the owner let him go since I was never contacted by anyone. In the end, a co-worker adopted the budgie. I had photos of him and she saw him and fell in love with him. She said he sang all the way home with her. I'm going to go over to see him in about a month and retrieve the cage as I might end up getting birds in the future now that I've seen how nice they can be.

The online personals are great though. Before I moved here from back east, I scoured the classifieds for an apartment. I ended up finding a place to live with someone I didn't know and we became best friends. Each of us just had a feeling that the situation was just right, so she rented to me having never met me. Then I had to find a job. I was able to find employment within a month of moving out here – once again off of the classifieds and the Internet. Now all I needed was a boyfriend. I posted an ad for someone to hang out with but didn't post a photo or a description. My mailbox was inundated with about a hundred emails in 24 hours. So many emails that I had to pull the ad. I went through them all and there was only one person that I responded to (who didn't include a photo either) and we exchanged emails. I'm not one for typical dates and he mentioned that he was driving down to see his folks in Los Angeles the following weekend. So I came up with the idea that we would go together and he would drop me off at my parents' house, which is on the way, and we'd get to know each other on the drive.

After telling his friends about this, they convinced him that I must be a man and urged him to meet me for coffee. So we met once for about half an hour. No real sparks but we decided to go on the trip anyway. After talking nonstop for six hours there and another six hours on the way back, we immediately decided to start dating each other and this lasted for about ten months. At that point, I had my apartment, job and boyfriend all from Craigslist. Then it got even better, because I got to meet Craig (*the* Craig) though my boyfriend. (Apparently they knew each other from when they were in college.)

I've also had people post for me a few times in Missed Connections. I tend to bolt from parties before allowing anyone to ask for my number. But another interesting story was when I had been reading postings on CL with regard to someone looking for help on finding a job.

They had listed all their qualifications and that they were going to pay a stipend for someone who helped them find a job. The next day I was out with my roommate and met up with this person she had met at her dance class. The woman started telling me about her job search and I said, "Did you post on Craigslist? I read your ad!" It was indeed her.

This was shortly after my breakup with the CL boyfriend and I ended up learning firsthand how small this city can be. It turned out that he had contacted her off of a dating site, not knowing that I had met her. So I was lamenting my failed relationship with this guy to her and she later e-mailed me, included a photo and asked, "Is this him?"

Boy I was pissed when I found out that he had e-mailed her less than a week after our breakup. Then again, online trolling *is* very easy.

# Honey, I confess and I'm sorry - m4w

Honey, I have a few confessions to make. I want you to know that I love you, and I hope you don't hold these things against me. We've been through some rough patches before, but we've come through okay. And look at us now. We have a beautiful home, two beautiful children, and our future together. Everything is fantastic, and it's only going to get better. Having said that let me confess these things:

You know how you said that your hot (your word, not mine) friend, Michelle, from the gym is in a better mood now that she's getting laid again? Well, you may have noticed that I'm in a better mood myself these days. Let's just leave it at that, shall we? Okay... deep breath here. Remember, I love you.

Also, do you remember when I went snowboarding the weekend of March 19th? I was going to go up with Reuben and Matt? You noticed that I looked remarkably un-sunburned after I got back. You said that you knew that I had fun because I couldn't sit downcomfortably for the following week. You asked if Matt and Reuben had a good time, and whether or not either of them could sit down -- kind of making a snide little joke. Well, they didn't go. Neither did I. I couldn't sit down because I spent those days at an all-weekend play party being the bottom for a woman named Mistress Luxor. I got spanked so hard that I had a difficult time even walking. I confess to that, hon. But if it's any consolation to you, after a weekend of licking boots, your home cooking was like a dream come true.

I love you, honey. I hope you can find it in your heart to love me back.

" I posted this rather over-the-top Missed Connections ad as a joke and had no real expectations from it. Ironically, someone actually responded to it and I ended up meeting a really cute, wonderful woman who turned out to be a supportive, inspirational friend. "

# "I DO LIKE TO TAKE CHARGE IN THE BEDROOM"

WOMEN SEEKING MEN

No plans for the weekend?

Me neither. Let's chat.

" I haven't really talked about what happened until now. It was back in the summer of July 2003. I posted my first ad and I wasn't really expecting that anything would happen. I received several responses but only one guy really caught my attention. He made his response short and straight to the point. So, I replied back with my cell phone number. I wasn't going to go out that night but he called me and wanted to meet. So, we met at this restaurant/bar in Cupertino. We had a great night, danced and talked and laughed. We ended up going to his place, and guess what? We lived in the same apartment complex! I spent the night with him, had sex all night long and the next morning.

The next day I woke, I left, gave him a hug and I thought that was it. It was one of those one-night stands that most people always want to try at least once.

The next day, I was at my friend's wedding and I didn't mention anything about what happened the night before. I didn't even really think about him. Next thing I knew, he started calling me and wanted to get together again. So, we did. We saw each other about three or four times a week, mainly sex, for the next two months. After two months of having a casual relationship, he started to take me around. I met his friends, co-workers, roommate and even his brother. I knew deep inside he knew that I wanted more than just a fuck buddy, but he ignored it. But I also knew deep inside that he cared about me as more than just that, but he was just too afraid to commit himself. We were still playing with fire for the next 4-5 months until, finally, one of us had to end it. I pretty much gave him an ultimatum that if he wasn't going to commit himself with one woman only, (which was me), then it was over. I found out middle of November that I was pregnant.

I knew right then and there that he would not want to have anything to do with me.

He wanted me to have an abortion, but I was raised as a Roman Catholic and I would not do that. He pretty much told me to get lost by December. It was the most difficult thing to do, but I knew that it was the right thing. Now, I'm better and much happier without him. I still think about him once in a while, wondering, "What if we were still together..." but I know I would just end up getting hurt again. Currently I'm living with someone who adores and respects me. We've been together for over seven months now and so far we are very happy. I actually met him online as well, in a chat room for Over 30's. Although I wasn't old enough to be in that room, we connected right away that first night, talked on the phone after two days, and the rest is history. 99

# Looking for something
# FUN — and REAL

Yes, dating is fun. Being a playful, intriguing, pretty, soul-
ful single woman in the city brings its share of rewards. Yes,
I meet a lot of guys and get asked out a lot. But I'm ready
for something more than just fun and surface and sweet. I'm
ready for something fun and deep and sweet. Something real. I
have friends who have had good luck on CL, so I thought, why
not check out all my options for meeting the right person,
both offline and online.

I'm 5'6, 120 lbs, slender but with the right amount of curves,
active social life, active physical life,   independent, easy-
going, night-owl, reader and sometimes writer, crafty, generous, sometimes sassy, love the outdoors, hiking, dance and
music, love to laugh.

If you are between 28-40 years old, comfortable, thoughtful,
warm, physically fit, attractive, have a great sense of humor,
politically liberal, environmentally conscious, sexy, in touch
with your emotions, and financially stable, then I'd love to
hear from you.

My physical type tends to be guys with dark or salt & pepper
short hair, between 5'9"-6'2", nice abs, great smile,
sparkling eyes, medium or larger than average nose, alternative style.

PLEASE TELL ME ABOUT YOURSELF, AND TELL ME WHY YOU RESPONDED
TO MY AD, WHY YOU THINK WE'D GET ALONG. Be real, be honest, be
interesting; don't just say, "Hi, you're beautiful, I'd love
to get to know you, blah, blah, blah..."

Please include at least one recent, clear picture in your
reply. NOTE: I WILL NOT RESPOND TO REPLIES WITH NO PICTURE
ATTACHED.

Bonus points for vegetarians and creatives!

If I think we would get along, I'll reply to you, and include
a full face and body pic of myself along with my reply. Fully
clothed of course.

" I was directed to the personal ads section of Craigslist by friends who've had successes there, and so I thought I'd give it a try and posted this ad in "women seeking men". I liked that it was free, anonymous and non-committal. I also liked that I could create my own ad style rather than having to use a cookie-cutter format like on a dating site.

My last serious relationship had ended a year before, and I realized I kept being attracted to, and ending up with, the same type of guy – creative, fun, exciting, smart, but emotionally unavailable. I tried to knock myself out of that, and dated somebody for a couple of months who seemed to be emotionally there, but I just wasn't into him. Then I went to Burning Man and ended up meeting another great guy – who also ended up being the same type as always. That's when I realized that I needed to break out of my pattern and consciously put it out there that I wanted something emotionally deep – a serious, committed relationship. Someone out there who I could imagine really wanting to be with for the rest of my life, even though at the time, I didn't think marriage was in the cards for me. I thought it would never happen. Then Joel came along. :)

He was one of over 200 responses I received from my ad, many of which were a complete waste of time. I narrowed it down to twelve that I replied back to via email. I was very thorough and methodical – I had a feeling I was making a very serious life decision, and so I was taking the process seriously. From the twelve, I narrowed it down further to three to go on first dates with. After our initial contact on Craigslist, I felt very comfortable with Joel right away over our first few email exchanges, which led to a couple of phone conversations and eventually our first date at a local wine bar. It was wonderful, comfortable and fun. We laughed easily together and talked for hours until the bar closed. Joel asked me out on a second date during our first date. On my drive home, I saw an incredible moon in the sky, and called him to make sure he saw it. That was a testament to how comfortable I already felt with him. I eventually chose to be committed to Joel and we started dating exclusively. A year later we celebrated our first anniversary as a couple in Paris. We walked to the Eiffel Tower from our hotel early one morning (2:00 a.m.), where Joel surprised me with an engagement ring and asked me to marry him. Five months later we were married in June 2008, and now I'm pregnant! I just found out today that it's a boy, and I couldn't be happier. I'm so glad I made the decision to go on Craigslist, because otherwise I don't think Joel and I would ever have met, and I'd still be in the same rut of dating the wrong guys for me! 99

# Frozen Eggs

Last great book I read: To Kill a Mockingbird. Most
humbling moment: When I lost the Miss America pageant.
Favorite on-screen sex scene: Behind the Green Door. Celebrity
I resemble most: I've been told I look a little like Gary
Coleman, but I don't see it. Best (or worst) lie I've ever
told: I love you. If I could be anywhere at the moment:
Accepting my Lottery Check in Tallahassee or lying under Hugh
Jackman saying, "I love you." Song or album that puts me in
the mood: Purple Rain. The five items I can't live without:
#1 = Vibrator, #2 = Dog, #3 = Cat, #4 = Bike, #5 = Toothbrush.
Fill in the blanks: ass hair is sexy; back hair is sexier. In
my bedroom, you'll find: a lot of batteries. Why you should
get to know me: Because Gary Coleman is hot.

I'd like to meet someone with a good sense of humor, a love
for the outdoors, sensitivity and a high sperm count (or at
least a love for Chinese babies).

66 This came to be one night when I had a friend over and we both created ads just as a joke. However, it has garnered some pretty interesting replies. I lost count but I've had close to 750 responses or more. Out of those, I'm meeting someone next weekend in Mexico for a four-day vacation/dive trip. (Definitely the most adventurous of my meetings to date!) I've also met people through chat rooms. One man from Boston IM'd me asking about Miami as he was to be moving here. This eventually turned into a relationship that lasted quite a while but fizzled due to being so far apart. Another man IM'd me out of the blue one day and we figured out that we lay out at the nude beach in North Miami within 30 feet of one another and said hello every weekend, yet had never met. We briefly dated but it's evolved into a fabulous relationship and we have been best of friends for about three years now. 99

# Ever considered being a father?

Natural beauty, slim, smart, financially self-sufficient, seeks mutually satisfying sexual relationship with unique man who will help me become pregnant. Three month minimum commitment desired. Long-term sexual benefits (and the economy of shared household expenses) if you want to move in and help me raise our child.

Ok, there. I did what you might have thought impossible. I wrote a completely original personal ad!

On the chance that someone will actually consider this proposition, let me go boldly forward with additional specs about me, and my hoped-for partner.

I'm over 35 and prefer same. In the past I've connected well with scientists, writers, engineers, teachers - and almost any type of intellectual iconoclast.

My personality is upbeat and unconventional, but I also like time to myself and value harmony and mutual support. My past boyfriends have been very handsome, and while I don't have specific looks criteria, sexual chemistry is important to me. I am thus definitely looking for a guy who, like me, is in good physical shape and plans to stay that way.

" I have always been the type of person who's willing to try new things and broaden my horizons. I think many people who use the Internet tend to be the same way – very progressive, forward thinking, intelligent, etc. It's becoming a great way to meet people and more and more men and women are catching on to it every day. You just need to be a little careful and aware of some of the protocols, etiquette, rules, etc., and exercise a little personal common sense and responsibility. I placed personal ads back in the 1980s and 1990s, back when it wasn't as acceptable. I never had a problem with it though, and I've met plenty of people this way over the years.

But the Internet has now taken things even further. You can place free ads online like this one and remain completely anonymous for as long as you like, or you can go the route of a dating site where you have to pay to be a member, but can include photographs, describe in more detail what you're looking for, exchange emails, etc. Both have their merits, and I've used them both to meet people, but I never thought, until recently, that I'd use them to meet someone to have my baby with.

For about four years I've wanted to try to get pregnant. Three successive boyfriends were unwilling to help. That was very painful. Although I could meet many men to date, it was a pain playing a game in which I tried to gauge how willing they might be to help me get pregnant soon – and as I turned 40 and then 41, I started thinking in terms of months instead of a year or so. I've been successful at work – indeed so much so that I bought a condo, have savings and a lot of job security, including very generous maternity leave. So I could get pregnant on my own. Still, my dream was to meet someone who would share the joys of raising children with me, right from initial conception, through to birth and on. My last boyfriend was very aware that I wanted to get pregnant and we had numerous discussions (arguments) about the topic, and even before I moved out, I began placing ads on an Internet dating site. I mentioned that I wanted to have children, but otherwise, my ad was fairly standard. I was shocked at the vast number of responses (and later learned from various men that any woman with a reasonably attractive photo would be inundated with responses). In a year, I received over eight hundred emails from people responding to my ad! You'd think this was a good thing, but one drawback was that many people only skimmed over what I was looking for. They were just responding to my photo more than anything. I eventually had to replace it with a less attractive one to weed out responders who were e-mailing mostly on the basis on a photo.

The filtering that you can exercise among the large pool of responders saves a lot of time, and allows you to more rapidly meet someone who could be a match. What surprised me was that I ended up, after about a year of rather normal dating via personal ads, placing a very unconventional ad – I specifically requested men who would be willing to help me get pregnant.

As a fallback I've scoped out the sperm banks, clinics, etc., but I really don't want to go that route if I can at all help it. I learned though some of my online friends in an online discussion forum that there are men out there who are willing to be known donors and help women like me out in these situations. After learning this, I did find someone who has agreed to do this with me as a last resort. I say that because I still really want what most women want – a friend/lover/partner/husband/father of my child. I wasn't quite willing to give up on my dream of finding that person just yet. There had to be someone out there who was right for me, and who wanted the same things I do. So, as a last resort I decided to place this rather extreme personal ad of my own online.

I didn't really expect to find anyone suitable, but at the very least I thought I'd have nothing to lose by putting myself out there one last time, and wanted to know that I've tried everything before having to make that phone call to my new sperm donor friend.

I was amazed to have received over 30 responses from interested men. Some were too young for me and some seemed more interested in the sex part than anything. But about 10 men were professionals, successful, articulate, well educated, interesting, slightly older (forties to early fifties) who missed out on having children themselves for whatever reason (previous marriage, too busy, etc). In a way, this was perhaps their last chance to meet someone who could be the mother of their children too, even though they are otherwise very successful and don't really have a problem meeting people or getting dates. One man noted that he figured I wasn't really serious about a man who would want to help me get pregnant, but that I was exaggerating for effect (to avoid dating anyone one didn't want to have children). But this guy did say he was open to having children at some point with the right person.

I found this interesting, because I was indeed serious, but also very motivating because this placed me into a new category – more of a "normal" dating situation where I might actually meet someone I'd like to otherwise date and eventually develop into a loving relationship – exactly what I was really hoping for.

In the end, I managed to get better quality responses from better quality men as a result of this more "extreme" type of personal ad than any other I've placed in the past. So perhaps that's the trick. I've met two people who have great potential from this ad posting (both doctors) and I'm getting to know them both. We haven't discussed my ad yet. I think we all want to act like this is a more "normal" dating situation for now as long as we still want the same things. But I think it's a little strange that no one has brought it up yet. Wouldn't you ask why I'd place such a strange ad? I guess I'll just have to see how this all plays out.

I do know this though. I would never want to return to a world without Internet dating, where you have to rely on friends setting you up all the time, awkward dinner parties, going to bars, etc. I've found that you get to meet a much better quality of people online, who are generally more attractive, professional, educated and successful. You just need to know where and how to find them. **"**

# I know exactly who I want.

You are exciting, adventurous, a little devil, sexy, cute, in shape, FUNNY, smart, witty, wise, spiritual, open minded, self-confident (not cocky), creative, and NOT some boring-ass conservative guy who wears button up shirts and goes to lame sports bars. I love men who have dark hair/eyes and are fit. Mmmmm... I like developed arms... Men who are Pisces, Cancer, Virgo, or Gemini ONLY.

I am funny, wild, sexy, attractive, creative, sensual, passionate, smart, spiritual, fun, curious, a dreamer, active, educated. I'm 5'7 tall, long brown hair, green eyes, and fit.

If you match my description and like my description as well then I would love to hear from you.

" I actually put up this online ad as sort of an experiment and I got a TON of responses. Which made me think that men really do like the idea of a woman knowing what she wants. I didn't reply to any of them though. I have never dated anyone whom I have met via the Internet and probably never will. I think the chances of meeting someone truly compatible, and who isn't an axe murderer are remote. Whatever happened to bumping into someone special in the park? Or the supermarket, café or local library for that matter? Call me old fashioned or call me cheesy, but I am never going to resort to dating on the Internet.

When I posted this ad, I just got out of a horrible three-year relationship and wanted to just see what was out there. After getting all those responses to my posting, it freaked me out a bit and made me realize that I was not quite ready to meet anyone. They all basically said the same thing, "Oh wow, I love a woman that knows what she wants."

I thought that was pretty interesting because I don't think most women know that it is a real turn-on for a lot of men. I think if more women knew this, then that would kind of inspire them to really get in touch with themselves and figure out what it is that they want, instead of just focusing on a man's needs.

I used to be exactly the same way with my old boyfriend, but found that he just took advantage of me and that I was slowly losing my own identity. I felt so free after we split up, which was exactly one year ago, and I haven't had a date since. I really did not want to. But now I'm ready and want to date again. I want to meet someone who is exciting yet passionate, artsy, open-minded, and spiritual. Someone like me, but not too much like me I guess.

Oh yes, they must have a great sense of humor (otherwise forget about it) and they have to be the right star sign, namely Cancer, Pieces, Virgo, Sagittarius or Capricorn. No Aries or Leos men.

I know this probably sounds crazy, but I have done a lot of research on this. I've found that Leos are great as friends, but they may be too selfish in the relationship and the last thing I want is another one-way street again. As for Aries men, I just butt heads with them. They're too headstrong for me and I don't want anyone dominating me. The thing I do like and can relate to with an Aries though, is that they are all about self-discovery. But because I'm a Taurus baby and, as a result, am rather headstrong myself, I just don't see me dating an Aries very seriously for any length of time.

But aside from my little online experiment here, I have to say that I am very anti-Internet dating. I guess I'm just a romantic a heart (eyes meeting across a crowded room, having a crush on someone at work, love at first sight, etc.).

And it all frankly just seems so unnatural to me. Surely, there are other more traditional, romantic and safer ways for attractive, normal, busy people to meet other people these days, aren't there?

That said, I must say that I haven't had the best of luck meeting quality men through other means though. I don't know what it is. I am not one to brag at all, but people generally consider me to be very good looking and say I should be a model. And I like to think that I'm also a very nice, sweet person who's easy to get along with. I have a ton of friends and people to hang out with on the weekends, but when it comes to men it's all down hill and I just don't know that many single, STRAIGHT men in Boston.

Men at bars and clubs bore me and I'm not really up for one-night stands. I had one over the summer and it was just awful. I should have known better, but I did it just to make the gay guy who used to live with me jealous. (It's a long story, but he led me to believe he was bi-sexual and kept grabbing me, kissing and flirting with me every day. It was driving me crazy and I wanted him so badly! One day I couldn't take it any more and jumped into his bed naked as an April Fool's Day joke, but he just kicked me out.)

Anyway, the one-nighter guy ended up having a really small penis. He was the *third* guy I had to chuck away in a relatively short period of time because his member was way too small. I've had such bad luck with this! Needless to say, my attempt to make my roommate jealous obviously backfired on me.

There was this other guy at work who I had a brief fling with who wins the prize for having the smallest penis I have ever seen. It was three inches long at the most and extremely thin – like a pencil. I tried to work with what he had as best as I could, but he said that he was so intimidated by me that he just kept losing his erection. So not only did he have an extremely small dick, he couldn't keep it up either. And to make matters worse, he made me wait for it too.

He said he wanted to take things really, really slow with me – and now I know why! We dated for about a month and a half and still hadn't been intimate together. I'm all for taking things slow and all, but six weeks is a little too slow by most people's standards and it was driving me absolutely nuts!

Finally the "big" night arrived on New Year's Eve, and, as I mentioned, he failed to get it up and it ended in disaster . . . along with our relationship.

The only good thing about him was that he was passionate like me but just not as sexually aggressive. I think I scared the crap out of him actually. I need someone who has a high sex drive but is passionate and sexy too. I mean, I didn't exactly tie him to my bedpost and whip him or anything like that, but . . . let's say I do like to take charge in the bedroom.

So after dating all of these guys, (my loser ex-boyfriend who constantly ignored me included), I have come to realize as I re-enter the dating world what it is that I do, and more importantly, what I *do not* want in a guy: someone who's gay, has a small penis and is mean and cold to me.

I'm currently taking applications. Just not on the Internet.

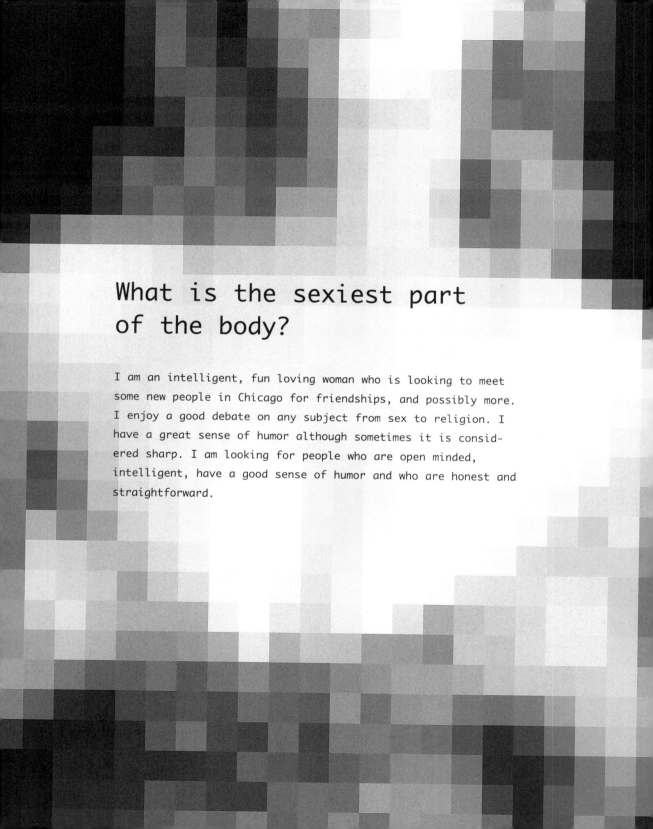

# What is the sexiest part of the body?

I am an intelligent, fun loving woman who is looking to meet some new people in Chicago for friendships, and possibly more. I enjoy a good debate on any subject from sex to religion. I have a great sense of humor although sometimes it is considered sharp. I am looking for people who are open minded, intelligent, have a good sense of humor and who are honest and straightforward.

" I have been married for twenty-one years. We recently opened our marriage due to some problems we were having. When I was thinking of ways to go about meeting new, intelligent people I figured most professionals would be using the Internet. Whereas at a bar, most of the time people are looking for a one-night stand and that is not what I am looking for. Overall, I've received 99% positive responses from my ad. Most are from men; not very many are from women. One reason I think most of my responses have been from educated men (doctors, lawyers, etc.) is that I emphasize intelligence in my posts, and not just sex.

I have met several people from my ads. All of them have been what I expected and none so far have been a disappointment as far as their personalities. Usually we'd go out on a few dates and if the feelings were mutual we would add sex to our relationship. I did have one situation that was a little uncomfortable though. I often get approached by men who live out of town and want to meet me while they are visiting for a convention or something. Occasionally I do. One time I agreed to meet with someone but informed him that I do not sleep with men from out of town. To make a long story short, I cut the date short and went home (the date was dull). Two days later I received a call from his wife asking if I met her husband while he was in town. I did know he was married, as are many of the men I meet online. I told her the full truth (but left out details that would only hurt her more). She said she had found his computer files and all the e-mails that he saved. I now rarely meet anyone from out of town.

But again, most of my online experiences really have been very positive. I've even started to date a transsexual, which I never would have thought of before. We love each other very much, but due to her situation we only see each other once a week. My attraction for her is who she is. I fell in love with her long before I met her. Her personality touched my heart fairly early in our correspondence and she was up-front with me. I was not looking for a relationship with a TS, but thought I would enjoy corresponding with her as a friend. The more I got to know her the more I forgot she was a transsexual and I just thought of her as her.

In general, I feel that online dating is a terrific way to get to know someone before meeting them. If done correctly, it is much safer and more reliable than meeting someone at a bar or even at work. And it's wonderful to be able to communicate and socialize with people from all over the world. 99

# Seeking true romance

I think the heading says it all! If you don't know what
romance is . . . then don't bother contacting me.

" I've met a few men over the Internet. Most of which were nice enough but were really just looking for sex. Oftentimes for an ongoing FWB arrangement, but some just wanted to meet as a one-time shot. I've also noticed that most of the men posting/responding to ads seem to be going through the seven-year itch thing. Nothing new there, except now you can see just who is going through it online! And it's not just men – there are also a lot of women that are experiencing it too, and at the same time, have hit their sexual prime.

Some of the men who contacted me became unsure about wanting to fool around and didn't know if they could stand the guilt of infidelity. Whenever I'd meet a man like that, I would encourage them not to enter into any such thing. Because if just meeting another women caused them feelings of guilt, then it would be a lot worse if they were ever to go through with it. But for the most part, most of the men I've encountered just wanted no strings sex, and only wanted it then and there. I was not looking for that, and with all the STDs out there I happen to be very careful about whom I have sex with, protected or not!

I did meet one man that was most wonderful. I was only with him twice, but we did talk on the phone and also exchanged a quite a few intimate e-mails and pictures. He was just a really wonderful man. We were going to meet a third time and then suddenly, all communications from him stopped. I was not sure what had happened to him, if he got sick or happened upon some bad luck or something. Then I started placing ads again since I figured I was not going to hear from him again. And lo and behold, he happened to be posting ads too. It is very likely that he never stopped when I did. But hey, to each his own.

It does hurt that he suddenly stopped writing and prefers not to communicate any longer. But that's his choice, and even though I have a bit of a broken heart from this situation, that is a known risk that we all take in meeting someone, whether it's through the Internet or at the local bar.

I've since met another man online and I continue to see him about once a month. This is a very good relationship between him and I. We meet at a romantic and discreet motel, which he pays for. And it is not a cheap fleabag place either. We spend most of the night together. Then I go home and he travels on until the next time he is in this area. He is a very considerate lover and for now it is all that I need. "

# Kinky librarian seeks tall vegetarian Latino

Bet that will get a lot of replies...but hey! A girl has to have her standards. I am 30 years old and dangerous with or without my glasses on....

" That was the first – and probably the last – personal ad I ever posted anywhere. Mostly because I got the feeling that the same creepy guys just respond to every single post, regardless of what it says. I had the naive idea that because I had asked for such a specific, and nearly oxymoronic, set of characteristics (although those *are* characteristics of my ideal man), I'd get one response, or maybe none at all. Instead, I seemingly received a sampling of the entire desperate male population. I was flooded with responses within a couple of minutes. Most guys had none or maybe one of the qualifications that I had listed, and many seemed super creepy. And most of the responses were not Latino, but figured they had a chance anyway. Fair enough, I guess, because I'm not actually a librarian. I just look like one. If I was a sociologist, I'd definitely study online dating, though it seems a ripe forum for analysis. "

# I Pick Fights

Twin powers activate into the form of an ice cube! Faster than a speeding fish! More powerful than a chain saw! Able to leap over huge holes in a plot. I have traveled to the ends of the earth and found that it really is flat in the two dimensional world. I laugh at the wind; blizzards are my friend. My imagination refuses to be tamed and I like it that way. I am not what you expect. I am a dark horse but look on the bright side of life. Curiosity is my motive. Ask me any question and I will give you a truthful answer. Where is your sense of adventure?

" Some people thought this posting was dark and morbid. It's interesting to see what people read into the things when they project their own voice onto my writing, or maybe they don't know that a dark horse is a positive attribute.

This was actually my third post. I'm a little new at this, so I don't have too many stories to tell. And until recently, I hadn't had any real "dates from hell" yet, and I didn't feel like a veteran dater until I had at least one of those. The closest one I had was this one fellow who responded to my post. We spent a week e-mailing back and forth the most witty and romantic line of questioning. When I asked him how I would recognize him if I saw him on the street he said by the note pinned to his shirt with my name. I said he would know I was near when the sent of vanilla was in the air. (It was a blind date.) We met for coffee and instead of the engaging back and forth conversation I was expecting from him, he just talked nonstop for two hours about his views, hardly pausing for a breath. Needless to say, I ended this painful date as soon as he ran out of breath.

And then it happened. The horror story I was expecting. I started corresponding with someone else who also had responded to this ad, and it led to some pretty interesting dates, including one where the police shone a spotlight into his SUV and over the bullhorn we heard the voice of disgust say, "Do you *have* to do that in public?" (We weren't even really doing much at that point.)

I thought he might turn out to be someone special but I kept somewhat guarded because it was too soon to tell if he was thinking the same thing, or just having conversation with me in order to get sex. We exchanged more than 200 extremely hot, steamy emails that started off with a seemingly innocent, "I have to go to the gym now and bend myself into a pretzel. Do you like pretzels? With salt?" We went out on a few dates together and fooled around. I was extremely drawn to him – like no man ever before. I was about to have lots of sex with him, and was willing to be just a friend with benefits, but I needed to know if he was having sex with anyone else for safety reasons. First he said he had another woman in another state. Then there was another close by. Oh, and yeah, there was a third woman . . . his wife!!!

He told me his wife doesn't like sex, which I find almost impossible to believe because they are both in their twenties and he is really good with his hands. I knew deep down that this was going to turn out this way from the very start, and yet I am strangely depressed. I so want to find someone that can prove to me that not all men are self-centered jerks looking for sex. But of all the guys I've dated, most of them have proven themselves to be self-centered and not really interested in what someone else has to say. Nearly half are only looking for sex and will say anything to get it. They'll pretend to be interested if they think it will increase their chances. Perhaps that percentage may be high because I'm currently only finding dates through the Internet and keep finding guys that just want one thing and think this is eBay for chicks. We are not e-tickets.

Anyway, I kept e-mailing this person back and forth as this led to a philosophical debate about why people do these things to each other. He, of course, has taken up the "guerrilla defense." My position was actually fairly nonjudgmental and I was really curious as to why he was willing to risk his marriage over his libido. That's why I had the ongoing debate instead of pure hatred for the guy. I'm still trying to understand men and why so many of them use and discard women. It's a big project.

After exchanging over two hundred really long emails to each other I'm still no closer to figuring this out. The debate eventually fizzled because it was going nowhere with our constant back and forth playing of point/counter-point and his feeble attempts at Jedi mind tricks. ("You want to have sex with me.") Thus confirming my hypothesis that he was just continuing the debate out of some hope that I'd get into bed with him. I just stuck to my guns and kept telling him to be good to his wife. Oddly, the experience actually helped me in some strange, twisted way to solidify my point of view that men really are led around by their penises. 99

# 31 yr old who looks 25 giving this a try...

Attractive, curvy, 31 year-old, techie-type girl who still gets carded all the time seeks someone who is 22-35, at least 5'10" and, of course, attractive. I'm not looking for anything too serious — just a little discreet fun for now, maybe a friend with benefits.

I would like to exchange photos before we meet, but I want to make sure we hit it off first before we go there. And please, while I'll definitely want to see it before we meet, please spare me the dick pics for now.

"I've posted a few times over the years, but nothing's come of it yet. I'm just trying this time around to meet some new people and maybe get a discreet friend with benefits. (I work in the entertainment industry and need to keep a low profile.) I was put off by some of the respondents who felt the need to send me a photograph of the bulge of their pants. Maybe it's me, but I just don't dig those things when I first meet someone. I want him to talk to me like a regular person first and see if we hit it off before the naughty stuff. I did respond to one personal ad recently though. It was for a threesome with two guys. They were both very nice and the conversation was interesting. I thought one of them was really attractive, yet I didn't want to offend or hurt anyone's feelings because I didn't want to sleep with them both. So now it's getting a little more complicated. Perhaps we are better off just staying friends. I just don't know!"

# Need a boyfriend

This island is too beautiful to experience alone. I've been here for three months and had very little contact with peers of the opposite sex. I would love to meet someone interesting to spend time with. Currently I am not working or looking for work so my time is fairly free. There is a chance that I'll be leaving in March so I'm not dead set on meeting the man of my life... just a close friend or romantic partner to spend lots of time with. Movies, dinner, hikes, basic daily stuff are my interests. Please be sincere and honest with a great deal of interest in getting to know someone new.

" I recently met someone here in Honolulu after being alone and basically dateless for three months. Our story is bizarre because it starts out where it probably should have ended up. We met and had sex on the first encounter, but now we hang out and go hiking and sightseeing with no sex to be had. The most important thing to happen in this man's company is sort of an uplifting story. I was sitting at a cafe at the North Shore with him and up walked a friend from college who I haven't seen in seven years. I wouldn't have been at the North Shore at that moment had he not invited me and picked that particular day. How wonderful . . . a great coincidence. "

# Are you taking off or landing?

I am just taking off! If you are as well, we might be able to fly together. Children are grown and on their own. Ended dead-end relationship and now want to fly! Looking for a friend, boyfriend, lover, escort, adventurer, maybe more. My dream guy is tall, strong, has position of power, loves to laugh, a great smile  and a twinkle in his eye. I prefer educated and cultured gentlemen with a daring side. I am attractive and experienced and eager. Would visit Vegas more if I had a reason to...

" I have found this to be a hot bed for horny married men just wanting sex. I have been too afraid of trying many of the wild offers and propositions put to me and the guys sometimes scare me off. When I feel free to talk uninhibited, then I am too embarrassed to actually meet them in person, so I rarely ever do. I did find two guys online recently whom I did meet though, and felt comfortable with. They were normal – one was married and the other a confirmed single guy – and weren't looking for anything too kinky, but both were a lot of fun.

I really enjoy letting loose and talking sexually online. It makes me hot and it's safe. It also gives me the freedom to be aggressive and adventurous and to act out secret fantasies in ways through email, IMs, etc., that I wouldn't normally ever do in person, and it's okay. "

# I am the best-kept secret in the Western World

MARRIAGE MINDED MEN ONLY

>>>>>>>>>>>>>>>>>>>>>>>>>>>>>>>

I am a highly educated, 42 y/o English-speaking Caribbean professional, non-US resident - no children, who simply wants to get married. An outgoing person,but I also enjoy family nights at home. I love big, tall guys, since I am 5'8". Have small children? I'd love to take care of you all. If you are an honest, patient, affectionate and highly intelligent man, and in need of a genuinely warm and loving woman, please reply, you'll be glad you did....

... and no... I don't want your money.

For those concerned as to why I am single at this age, I have been focused on getting an education and developing myself as a professional so as not to be dependent on a man for my sustenance (lol). I also happen to live in an island where there is a shortage of educated men.

66 I first started dating online in December, 2002. My experiences so far have been largely frustrating. I've met many liars and shallow minded men on the Internet who were all just after one thing. Most of whom were already married.

The presence of married men on dating sites really complicates issues for women who genuinely want to find a relationship. I am a busy person and have no time for bars or other social activities where singles mingle. So the Internet is the perfect place since I can do my searches at my leisure. It also helps broaden my range of possible dating partners, and before meeting someone I can determine if the person is worth my time. However, the phenomenon of cyber cheating has muddied the waters of online dating and made many of us genuine singles very defensive and has hurt many a spouse.

My first encounter was painful as I met a man who appeared gorgeous with a wonderful personality, who claimed to be a 44 year-old Army Colonel and trained psychologist. He said he was involved in Military intelligence activities, and as such told me that I would never find reference to him anywhere in the Armed Forces list of employees. On four different occasions he promised to visit me, but each time at the last moment claimed to be called away on an assignment or a personal endeavor. I tried to be understanding, but one day I got the urge to investigate him.

He sent me flowers on Valentine's Day through the Internet as I was living outside of the USA at the time. I was able to track down the name of the florist and spoke with the owner. After realizing that I had found myself in a bad situation she willingly provided me with a lot of information to help me in my search. It turned out that he was a

61 year-old married man who was trying to lure women to have affairs with him. His State denied that he was ever registered as a psychologist. I then realized that the photo that he sent me was a fake. I have since seen him post other personals using the same stolen photographs. I can attest to locating a woman from the Philippines and from Nigeria with whom he played this game. He became abusive when he discovered that I had uncovered his duplicity. Go figure.

The latest incident involved a man from South Miami who answered my ad. I was completely unaware of his marital status until I checked some public databases, simply on a whim. I was quite specific as to my requirements for a long-term relationship. He indicated that he was a single father divorced for two years with custody of his two sons. We developed a friendship first then he expressed a romantic interest in me. I told him early on that if he were a married man then I would have nothing to do with him. He insisted that he was divorced, and that he and his wife had "drifted apart." As I travel often on business, I invited him to meet me as a friend first since I prefer to get to know a man before getting physically involved. During our interactions he spoke often of his desire for me. However, on two occasions he declined my invitation to meet me, citing pressure of work.

I became suspicious and visited several public databases, made a discreet phone call to a number that was associated with him on one of the databases, and discovered his voice greeting with reference to a wife and children. Of course, he was still married! I was crushed, for I am no home wrecker and I confronted him with my findings, upon which he verbally abused me for invading his privacy.

Marriage and property records, along with telephone listings, are actually public information and a single woman has the right to investigate any man whose actions appear suspicious. These records are public knowledge for a reason and are often a good place to start since husbands and wives, if still married, often have joint listings.

I've since become a member of an online group that is against cyber cheating and am one of its few single women. It consists of suffering spouses (mostly wives and girlfriends) whose partners have been involved in online affairs while still married to/involved with them.

I guess I was one of the lucky ones. But really, why should I be required to check the county marriage records each time I meet someone I could be interested in? It's just not right. "

# are you my silver fox?

I've got a huge crush on my boss's boss. Come to think of it,
I've had a thing for a tall, lean, silver-haired genius
authority figure at my last several jobs. Do you cut a dashing
figure? Do you have a flinty, penetrating gaze? Would you fix
it on me through half-closed eyes, like you're picturing me
naked? Can you talk to me, in a deep, commanding voice, about
something in which you are the definitive authority? Okay,
that's too much. Something you're passionate about? Preferably
with your big, commanding, passionate hands on my body? Since
we can't have a private mentoring session in your office,
maybe we could meet for drinks and then you could blind me
with your brilliance and then you could suggest some other
nice place where you could, um, mentor me? I am a pretty,
thin, whip-smart young lady in need of some deft, skilled,
expert attention. Tell me a little about your area of
expertise. If you would even consider sending me a dick pic,
you are clearly not the classy brainiac I'm looking for. So
just to be clear: NO X-rated pictures please. A G-rated one
would be welcome, and reciprocated soon, if you sound
promising.

66    A few months ago I finally got up the nerve to respond to some ad posts, and put up one of my own. Since then I've been having SUCH HOT SEX with such a cool variety of interesting men! People I would never have met otherwise. None of the men I've actually met up with are remotely like what I described here in my ad, but it's what I thought I wanted at the time. It turns out that being brilliant and commanding isn't enough to make up for being 55 and not terrifically attractive. Anyway, it's what started everything.

Let me clarify first off that I am a normal girl. I have great friends and I'm close to my family. I have a really good, demanding job, and I'm starting a new one across the country in the Fall. I've never dallied in Internet sex before the last few months. But I broke up with my long-term boyfriend and really wanted attention and sex with someone (several someones actually) that I had never slept with before. And I figured that I was leaving town soon, so this was a good time for it. Most of the postings, and the responses that I got, were sketchy and horrible, but there were enough interesting ones to make me think that there were normal men out there online too.

So in total I met with four men. The first one I dated was 31 (I'm 22) and was clear that he wasn't looking for anything serious. He doesn't look or act much older than me. The first time we met, we went for ice cream, went to his house, smoked some weed, and had sex. The funny thing about him is that since that first time, we've had long flirty phone conversations, gone to the movies and held hands, hung out at his house watching a movie – basic date flirty stuff. It's just funny that it started happening AFTER we had sex. I've met up with him four times, and had good sex every time. He's my favorite, I think, because he seems to like me the least among the others (typical perverse challenge-seeking). He doesn't NOT like me; he's just the least demonstrative with his affection. I think about him the whole day after we hook up and save his voice mail messages to obsess over.

The first-sex-then-dating thing is actually true for bachelor No.2 as well. He's 34. The first time we met, we went for margaritas and then went to his house and had sex. We've had sex three nights so far. It's hard for me to take him seriously because he's really earnest. This is going to come off as bitchy, but I may as well admit it: he's a vegan environmental activist, and he wears flannels. I'm sorry, but I need a little more cynicism and style. I like him way better naked. We have excellent sex, at least twice every session. Anyway, he's really emotional, and he has an ex with whom he's still emotionally involved. But he also talks about how wonderful and sexy and brilliant I am, and kind of acts like we're dating. Last night I met some of his friends (so weird and mortifying) AND slept over at his house – both things that he's been inviting me to do since the first time we met, but I haven't been interested. And it's definitely not typical of a casual relationship thing (or at least of what I think of as one).

The third man is 37. He responded to my ad and we went for extremely expensive sushi and we kissed, but he was sooooo boring that I could barely keep a not-bored expression on my face during dinner. I wasn't attracted to him so I said I had to go home. The following day I wrote him a "No-Thanks" email. Poor guy; he was totally surprised. I wanted to give him a chance by having dinner and kissing (even though my instantaneous reaction to him was that I wasn't going to sleep with him), so I may have led him on a little.

My experience has been that I know whether I want to sleep with the guy I'm meeting in the first split-second I see him. I've gotten a photograph every time, and they were all real, but it's so hard to tell much from pictures – they all looked so different in person. In the first ten to twenty minutes of meeting the men I've met, I blush furiously and can't meet the guy's eye because I can't believe what I'm doing (and because I've already made up my mind to have sex in that first split second), but then I relax and have a good time.

With man number four, I still use my fake name with him as he's the most casual of the men I'm seeing. He's 40, lives in a fancy loft, has a glamorous job, plays edgy music for me, plies me with wine and fruit, talks super dirty, leaves all the lights on . . . generally it's all about the seduction and sex. I only go there in the early evening, after work, and I only stay to have sex and then I leave. The first time we met, I met him in a bar across the street from his house. We had two drinks, went back to his house and had amazing sex. I've met with him four times so far. The cool thing about him is that it's so far removed from my real life. I can't imagine meeting his friends or sleeping over, for example. Nor would I want to. I get to show up, get ravished and worshipped, leave, and fantasize about it for days. It's really fun. It's cool how I have so many people and sextastic events to fantasize about.

Up until recently, I haven't told anyone about any of this, so it's like I have this secret sexy alter ego, which is really fun. But this weekend I finally told two of my friends all about all these men. I chose, of course, to tell my more open-minded friends. They both had the same response: initially shocked into hilarity, but then, "Ah, why not? You're going through a tough, atypical time; this is a great way to rebound, as long as you have a healthy attitude about the casualness of the sex."

I may introduce my favorite man to a friend or two at some point, but probably not. I'm still feeling some embarrassment concomitant with all this Internet-mediated dating/sex stuff, and I'm just coming out of a relationship and not really willing to deal with dating/sex in a real-world plane. But I think that stigma is gradually lessening.

In my case, I don't mean that the stigma is so much about this being via the Internet, but that it's so blatantly casual. This may make me unusual for my age/gender/socioeconomic position, but I don't think that explicitly non-romantic sex is inherently dirty or sleazy. It's definitely fun to reinvent yourself vis-à-vis the sensual attentions of a worshipful man, which hinges on the casualness of it all, but it's not sleazy. **„„**

# MOC

Single, white, intelligent, reasonably sane and entirely
personable female has given up on love and decided to offer a
MOC to an equally sane and personable male who is in need
of/desires U.S. citizenship or has any other valid (by my
standards) reason for seeking a MOC. This offer is entirely
serious. I should mention, however, that I am currently living
in Europe, but that should be the least of our problems.

Although this is essentially a business deal, there obviously
has to be some level of attraction to make it work (thinks
me), so please send a picture with your response and tell me
what you "propose." As for me, I'm between 5'7 and 5'8, 140,
dark hair, attractive . . . anything else you'd like to know,
just ask.

Thanks for reading and good luck with your search,
wherever it may take you.

❝ I haven't exactly given up on dating. I just don't believe that it can (in my particular case) lead to love. In fact, I've dated quite a lot in the past several years. The problem is that I am already in love . . . with a married man. This does not bother me. The fact that he loves his wife (although he doubts that she reciprocates his feelings) and will not initiate a divorce for societal reasons, is likewise not a problem. Even if she were to request a divorce (which he would not fight), it is unlikely that our relationship would change significantly. But enough about this unfortunate state of affairs. I am not looking for love because I already have it. Without, however, actually "having" it. He is on the East Coast; I am in Germany. Granted, this minor glitch is "curable," but there doesn't really seem to be any need to address it for now. Thus, I am essentially single and available. But my heart isn't. So I date around when the urge strikes. I don't generally go in search of dates; they tend to just find me.

Last summer, however, a very unhappy chain of events led me to take matters more into my own hands. I'm not sure where I first learned about online dating sites, but I browsed through a few profiles and shortly thereafter created my own. My first encounter through one of these sites was with a 60-year-old Canadian who, after just a few lines of conversation, said that he'd really like me to come to Canada and live with him. I might note here that my online profile really is not all that detailed, and it certainly doesn't mention anything about looking for someone to marry (this was long before I came to the idea for the marriage of convenience) or an interest in moving halfway across the planet. So I very politely explained that I am fairly content to stay put for now, and I didn't hear another word from him.

Amidst various other brief and unpromising e-mail exchanges, I met (in person) a couple of men who were either in my area or passing through and had a good time with them, but nothing more. Then came "the big one." Literally. His profile stated that he was "a few pounds overweight" which is generally not my idea of a good time, but the extended chat sessions and e-mail exchanges were fun and interesting and there was clearly a connection on several levels. So despite the pictures that showed that he was well beyond "a few pounds overweight," (I never asked for specific numbers, but we're talking about some 300+ pounds on an approximately 5'9" frame), I bit the bullet and went to meet him in America. (He lived in the Midwest.) I stayed with him for a week and we got along fine, but I knew fairly quickly that he was never going to capture my heart. Unfortunately, I am very bad at telling people (guys) things that I am certain they don't want to hear, so I didn't say anything. And after all, I was going to be safely 5,000 miles away from him, so I felt I could get away without hurting his feelings too terribly. This, of course, did not work out quite as well as I might have hoped, and he is still trying to convince me that I clearly have more feelings for him than I am willing to admit.

Then an old friend of mine who now lives on the West Coast

with his wife of four years, whom he met on some other Internet dating site, pointed me to a job ad that he'd seen on Craigslist, thinking it might interest me. That was my first encounter with the site. I wandered around the site for a while and quickly became addicted. I began reading the online posts every day, just out of curiosity. There seemed to be little point in responding to them due to the distance and, of course, the fact that for 99.9% of malekind my heart seems to be buried under countless leagues of arctic ice. So I read on, enjoying the stories, sometimes admiring the creativity and humor, sometimes pitying the poor slobs who appear to be on a very different page than a good 80% of humanity. (But who am I to judge?) And very often cringing at the inability of huge swaths of the American population to make proper use of their mother tongue and its grammar and spelling rules.

Among the many ads I read were some looking for a marriage of convenience, usually for foreigners trying to get a green card. I don't know just why this particular concept got my wheels turning, but it did. I thought about it for several weeks before actually acting on it. I was *not* looking for love or any kind of relationship that might lead to love, but was offering a deal, plain and simple, that was open to some degree of negotiation. I assumed that most would suggest monetary compensation, but I did not want to discourage anyone by mentioning an explicit figure an "applicant" who could offer. For example, decent living arrangements in Hawaii might have appealed more than one who would pay $10,000 for me to live with him in a shack

in Mississippi. I thought I might, at the very least, get an interesting experience out of it (and am well aware that it could just
as easily go awry somewhere along the way) and help someone
out in the process. I fully expected to get some twisted responses, and I was not disappointed, but it could have been much
worse. I received 36 responses so far and more are still trickling
in from London.

A few people tried to encourage me to not give up on love. A
few others kindly pointed out that my "proposal" could well be
illegal. I also received a number of replies from people who
were apparently out to respond to every single post to improve
their chances of getting a reply, as their messages had absolutely no relationship whatsoever to my personal ad. Of the remain-
ing twenty-some, I exchanged multiple e-mails with about a
third, clarifying details and such, but at some point they all just
stopped writing. At least four of these seemed genuine and seriously interested, but I figure the fact that I am in Germany poses
an extra, unwelcome obstacle since I'm not local and it's probably too much hassle for most people. I work for myself, so I am
really quite flexible and can do my work from just about anywhere, but it's obviously not the same as if we could just go talk
about things over coffee somewhere down the street.

I would have seriously gone through with this with any of those
respondents who clearly saw the offer as a temporary business
deal and not a path to skip the dating scene and move right in
with a ready-made wife. Which is where many of the men who

responded were apparently hoping to go. I didn't expect this because I thought the ad was pretty clear about what I was offering. But I suppose that, in some sense, their idea would also fall under the definition "MOC." I politely replied to these men and told them that it was not my cup of tea. Most let it go at that, but one guy replied with a picture of himself with a woman (in a pose that would not likely get past a porn filter) just so I knew "what I was missing out on." Another still tried to convince me to give him a chance and felt it necessary to mention that along with being 6ft. 4in, athletic, never married, no kids, non-smoking and a non-drug user, he likes to drink like a fish, is horny as hell, adores giving oral, is into restraint, domination and submission, Japanese rope work, role playing and spanking. He gave me his phone number and dared me to call him if I was actually genuine. (I passed.)

So the search goes on. I have also begun to respond to other ad postings just to see what else might be out there for me despite the near-hopelessness of the distance and my cold heart, etc., and I've had some fairly enjoyable (but clearly going nowhere) exchanges in the process. Meanwhile, I guess I'll still keep looking for my MOC for now . . . and pining after my married man from afar. 🌸🌸

# sexy italian girl needs a boyfriend!

I'm a very outgoing ex pro cheerleader looking for a great guy! I'm attracted to tall white males who are outgoing, fun, non-flaky, established, college grad, basic well-rounded guys. Common interests... golf, tennis, outdoor sports, fine dining, jazz, basic lifestyle for adventure! I'm 5'4, blu/brn, curvy figure. Your pic gets mine!

" I'm 45 years old, never married, and have no kids. I live a full life and I've had some very good long-term, committed relationships over the years, but I've never found "the one" to eventually settle down with. I've met a lot of great guys I would have married, but alas, no one has asked me. I eventually turned to the Internet to help me find someone compatible because that's how people meet these days. I had high hopes, but in the end, I've been pretty disappointed.

Don't get me wrong – I've met a lot of people this way (online). I've had more than a hundred dates over the past four years (sometimes juggling two a night) through dating sites and the free personal ads. But making a relationship out of dating after meeting only a few times has been hard. Most of the men I've met were just after sex, into casual dating or just didn't want to make the effort. Men will be men I suppose, and I'm a very sexual person too, but I need more than that. I want a relationship. Instead, I keep encountering people who just want to get in my pants. And not without a whole lot of grace or subtlety I might add.

One guy I met about a year ago said to me after a couple of cocktails, knowing that I used to be a cheerleader, "Hey, I can do a cheer for you: DAMN, YOU'RE HOT!" This was followed by, "Why don't we just go and have sex, and *then* get to know each other?" Ummmmm, thanks, but no.

Another gentleman I met was 30 and liked the fact that I was an older woman. He liked this *a lot* apparently. We met for drinks and had a pretty good conversation. He eventually asked me if I wanted to go to his place (which was close by) and have a nightcap, watch a little television, etc. I normally wouldn't do such a thing on a first date, but thought what the hell, and told him okay, but that I'd only come in for a little while. We get to his place and he offers me a glass of wine and we settle down in front of the TV. After a little time passed, he says, "So you're actually 45? You look a lot younger." I assure him that I am, and a few minutes later he starts getting all excited and squirmy, gyrating his hips and pelvis . . . kinda weird behavior without actually touching me. Then he moved next to me, started putting his hand on me and trying to pull me in even closer to him. This was a little much for me and I put my hand on his shoulder and started pushing myself away.

"What are you doing?" I ask.

"Just give me a minute . . ." he says.

When I was finally able to move away from him,

I noticed that his friggin' zipper was down, and the next thing I know, *his penis comes flying out!* I just started laughing at it and the absurdity of the situation and ran out the door. I guess I should take it as a compliment that he found me so attractive and all, but that's not something I really want to see right away on a first date.

Not everyone is like this of course and this is an extreme example. I've met some great guys and I believe that there's a right person out there for everyone. I'm just older and picky about whom I want in my life. You'd think there's something wrong with me, but I'm actually quite good looking and fun. Men are just picky about falling in love and more able to treat sex casually. So you have to be careful these days, especially when going out on over 100 dates, because the ones that seem genuinely nice and interested in me, once I decide to let my guard down and sleep with them,

I never hear from them again. I must have a sign on my forehead somewhere that says, "Use me." I can't see it, but others obviously do.

This is true for the free personal ads as well as the paid dating sites, which I also experimented with for a while but stopped because it was too much work and got to be too expensive. I think when you belong to those sites, because you're paying a monthly fee, you feel obligated to get the most from your money. And so you invest a lot of time and effort writing your profile, exchanging emails, searching for people you might be compatible with, and you go out on as many dates as possible. But frankly, this gets laborious and I don't feel that I should have to pay to go out on a date with someone. Love should be free! And while every man on those sites claim that they want to have a relationship, they never do. In the end, they're just looking for sex too. 🙶

# Are there any left wing, smart-ass, BBW lovers here?

Slightly bored, dirty old woman seeks horny bad boy to jiggle the fat. Also good if you can utter complete sentences and take directions.

Me: divorced, no kids, Caucasian, creative type, open-minded, foul mouth.

You: SINGLE, over 35, not allergic to pet hair, know how to floss your teeth and wash your ass (not necessarily in that order).

Expect to eventually send a pic. Good luck out there.

" I am in my fifties, divorced and a BBW. Where else am I going to meet somebody? I don't like going to bars and I don't work outside of my home, so my options are rather limited. A couple of gay friends of mine said that you can find anything you want on the Internet and that there were lots of people out there looking for big beautiful women. This turned out to be true.

I've been dating online now for over two and a half years and have met about fifty people as a result. Some were fun, some scary and some of these people turned out to be great friends. I actually met my best friend on the Internet. I've experienced almost every kind of imaginable situation, but I still haven't found a life partner yet. And I don't think I'll find it on the Internet, frankly. Most people are just looking for a quick fuck and are not LTR material. And most of these aren't even single or available and are cheating on their wives, girlfriends or whatever. If you have an open relationship that's one thing, but I won't put up with liars. I've been getting better about weeding these people out though. For starters, they have to give me their phone number where I can call them at any time so that I know they are legit. I had this one guy who gave me a number that turned out to be a restaurant pay phone, and he would wait there for me to call. During our one and only conversation, the operator eventually cut in and said that we had to deposit some money into the phone or get off the line.

I also don't respond to people who send me one line emails in response to my ads, like, "Yeah baby, let's do it," (and they're usually misspelled). I can post a provocative ad and get 300 responses from it, easily. And I'm an old fat woman! Also, I'm very liberal and I don't fuck Republicans.

Politics are an important part of my life. I'll ask them where they lean politically and I tell them up-front that I'm left wing. If they're a Republican, I tell them they don't have a chance with me. I get a lot of hate mail because of this, but it does save some time and hassle in the long run.

The rest is just a matter of taking the time and making the effort of exchanging emails, photos, phone calls and eventually meeting up with those who seem like they might have some potential. Although in the end, I usually find myself disappointed because they've either lied about their appearance or sent a photo that wasn't recent (one guy actually sent me a 20 year old photo), lacked any kind of social skills or there just wasn't any chemistry between us. All you can do is to try to remain positive and hopefully the odds will eventually work in your favor that there's someone out there for you that's actually worth a shit. "

# Ode to Internet Dating

Dear sweet, loving computer-o-mine,
How I love the way you chime upon morning's boot-up.
The way you go directly to my e-mail inbox and provide
me with the joy and sorrow of each day's e-bounty.

How I love the way you provide me with endless
possibilities for love and disappointment upon every
dubious response and every e-mail describing my possibly future
ex-boyfriend of the day.

From Match.com to Yahoo Personals to Craigslist alike,
I see the men who come into my e-life with promises of
romance and love if I succeed the mutual match test
and am willing to forfeit my measurements and deny my
devious nature.

Ode to Internet dating and that first instant message.
Remembering who HotGuy246593 is and what he likes to do 'for
fun'. Ode to meeting for 'coffee' or a 'drink' at   my favorite
bar where people are starting to sneer and snicker. Ode to second
dates where I have to put out because you bought me dinner.

And Ode to doing it again in the hopes of 'something
better'.

The love just keeps on flowing my sweet personal counsel, from
the moment I post as the sweet, young (24), non-thin, non-freak,
drug-free, dorky lady that I am, to the replies and replies and
replies of photo-less cut-and-paste emails of boys at work, looking to kill time, or get laid or fall in love.

I look forward to these moments from that morning chime to the
inevitable shut down each glorious day.

"  Responses to my Ode included a guy look-ing for "mutual fun or casual pleasure," another who told me to get offline and go to a sports bar, someone who was into cuddling and watching movies and emphasized his loyal nature, and an email exchange that resulted in an argument about the difference between men and boys and how I was probably looking for the latter. This conver-sation bored me, as this guy was rather pretentious and unromantic. I also heard from someone whose whole response was simply, *"You don't necessari-ly have to put out on the second date."* To which I did not bother to reply. I have written many interesting ads, and tend to reuse them from time to time. I have been on many dates and have had a few short-lived romances . . . but that's about it. It keeps me amused and sometimes makes me feel good. Just another addiction I suppose. "

# Looking for Mr. Nice

I'm a mid-western girl looking for an affectionate, loyal,
kind, fun loving man. I love the beach, music, reading,
decorating my home, etc., all the usual things.

Please be confident, sure of what you want (most of the
time) and willing to allow me to nurture and spoil you.
You also need to eat my baking/cooking and pretend you
like it! The other thing I ask is that you believe in God,
as religion is an important part of my life.

I'm open to anyone 38-45, living within 25 miles of me,
caucasian, black or hispanic. Can't wait to hear from you!

" I have been married and divorced twice now. My first husband had an affair when our son was just six months old and I left him. I was only 24 at the time. My second husband and I gave it a good ten year try and have one wonderful son together, but sadly we couldn't make it either. Our divorce was final in 1998.

So since that summer I have been officially "single." Because of all the drama and pain of two divorces and being apart from my kids every other week between two different dads, I felt I would never find (nor even deserved) a man whom I could have a healthy, lasting relationship with. I wrote men and marriage off as something I just wasn't good at and that God must have other plans for me. But the loneliness and desire to have a companion remained.

So I worked on myself, learned all I could about my mistakes and how a healthy relationship should look. I bought my own place, changed to a more lucrative job, created new friendships, developed hobbies and personal interests outside of my "mommyhood" and focused on getting strong, well and being the best mom I could be. After three years of doing that I gradually realized I had created a life I loved, was independent and capable, didn't "need" anything, yet still wanted a man to love and share time with. I was still resolved never to marry again but I wanted a relationship nonetheless. I liked myself again and felt whole again. I've learned that this is the only way to enter into a healthy relationship – as two wholes; not two halves!

I started being more open to men who approached me, let my friends set me up, etc., but had no luck. I saw an ad for a dating site and decided to try that route. I started out just e-mailing – too scared to meet unless I've e-mailed for two weeks, then I'd arrange for a phone call or two before meeting for coffee/lunch or dinner. I didn't want to rush into anything and felt weird about doing the online thing anyway! I'm your basic Minnesota girl and my parents didn't know that I was even doing any of this. :-)  After almost three months of dating this way, I started getting really depressed. I was putting myself out there, going on a lot of dates and had no trouble getting attention, but no one was right for me. I knew exactly what I preferred and didn't want to just latch on to someone just for the sake of it.

My last day before my free membership expiration came up I decided not to continue, and with a heavy heart decided to resign myself to being single, but took one last look to see if there was anyone new online . . . just in case.

And there was Daniel! I'd seen his photo a million times. I loved his eyes and I would look at his photos but never wrote to him. I doubted a single guy, never married, no kids, in great shape, successful in his career, etc., would want to date a 40 year-old Mom, divorced twice with two sons from different men. I didn't sound real good on paper.

But he lived in my town and I knew it was my last day, so I wrote to him and just complimented him on his beautiful eyes and left it at that. He wrote back right away and we exchanged a few emails. I told him my free membership was expiring the next day, so we exchanged our personal emails. We both agreed that the drawn out process was not the way to go and so we decided we should meet and get it over with.

We met for coffee on a Thursday night. No strings for either of us if we didn't click. I arrived first and got a table. He walked in the door and didn't see me at first so I was able to check him out. He was gorgeous in person (even better than his photos) and I was immediately attracted to him. He turned and saw me and asked if I was Shelley. When I answered yes, he looked up at the heavens and said, "Thank God . . . *finally* someone who looks like their photos and even better." We both laughed knowing just what he meant and gave each other a quick hug.

So we started yapping away, sharing stories, laughing, and staring at each other. But I still dreaded having to tell him my history. He asked me if I was seeing anyone else, etc., and we started sharing our 'love life' pasts. His was a broken engagement and a series of woman who just didn't work. No big dark secrets, but an admitted pickiness that had kept him single. So I told him mine and after I was done I thought, "Okay, now he'll say he has to go and I'll never hear from him again."

He went to use the restroom and I got my keys out of my purse expecting him to let me down nicely and leave. Instead he sat back down and said, "I need to tell you that I was just in the bathroom pinching myself to be sure I'm not dreaming. How did I get so lucky to meet this beautiful, smart, funny, sexy woman?"

I could NOT believe my ears! My past meant nothing to him. He judged me for me and the present and the future! We continued to talk until the waitress tapped me on the shoulder to tell us they were closed. We'd been there for over four hours and didn't even know it. He walked me to my car and it was then we realized we lived two blocks from each other and had been neighbors for twelve years – minutes from one another and we never crossed paths. So he hugged me (a longer one this time) and I literally melted. I have loved men before, but I never felt *that* feeling before – like I'd found *him* at last. It was eerie.

I floated home on cloud nine and told my boys all about him. I also told them he is black and they had absolutely no worries or concerns over that, so onward I went. I told my mom the next day, "I think I just met the man I'm supposed to be with."

Ironically (I think it was God) a friend of mine said to me a few weeks earlier that the man that is right for me would have my name written all over him and that I'll just *know* and he'll know too. I hung onto that because I really wanted to *know* and to have that reciprocated to me 100%. I wanted to wait for that special one even if it meant being alone longer.

Well, my nickname growing up was ShellBell – no biggie until he told me his last name is BELL! So I was tickled that my name 'was written on him' and squirreled that little secret away. We then had our first official date a few days later and I got to see his home. He gave me a tour and said he wanted to show me something. We went to his bedroom and above his bed was a black & white drawing of a white woman standing with her arms folded across her breasts with red lipstick and her hair pulled back. Her face looked JUST like me. He said he was hoping to find someone like his drawing and he felt it was me! I then told him my "ShellBell" thing too and we giggled like fifth grade girls. The next night we saw each other again and we kept finishing each other's sentences, thoughts, and had such a connection that neither of us could believe it. We were both 40 and have been around the block enough to know who/what we wanted and didn't want. He kissed me and that was *it*.

Not that we didn't have our ups-and-downs and bouts of insecurity along the way, but we worked through them and he eventually proposed to me. I am totally in love with him and I'm looking forward to our upcoming wedding in June. I'm so happy we found one another . . . even in such an unconventional way! I've urged other single people to try it as well. I met so many different types of men and learned so much from them. I got a lot of practice with my communication skills and a new sense of confidence from all the sweet comments I received. It renewed my faith in men and I found out they have all the same worries and insecurities and need for love that I do.

# "WE BARELY MADE IT UP THE STAIRS"

:-X

CASUAL ENCOUNTERS

# Purr Kitty

I am a successful professional - sane, healthy and financially secure woman. I am also very happily married except for one issue: my husband's sex drive is nowhere near that of mine. However, this is not a problem, since neither of us believes in complete monogamy. Therefore, I am looking for men who either intend to remain single, or are also in a similar steady relationship. I REALLY do NOT go for the S&M/dom/sub thing. If you are looking for a top/bottom/switch, please look elsewhere. What I am is a sensualist. I love having my senses flooded. For me, music, cologne, massage, touching and tasting are the frosting on the cake we call sex. I am also very playful in bed. I think sex is and should be fun (as long as it is safe, sane and consensual). It is a basic pleasure of life and body. I pity people who do not understand this - what they are missing! I walk 8 miles a day, six days a week. I also take salsa, swing and aerobic classes. I have large breasts, but they are what Mother Nature gave me. I do not have a perfect Hollywood body, and I never will, but needless to say, I am in good shape. I don't expect you to have a perfect body, but I do prefer people who take care of themselves - better endurance. ;-) Finally, I am a *very* discreet and private person, and I will never invade your private or professional life in any way.

I'd love to hear from you if you're a man who is sane, healthy and secure, single or is already in a steady relationship, isn't domineering, has a great sense of humor, in good shape, likes curves (this baby's got a D cup and a decidedly feminine behind), is discreet and respects my privacy, and knows and insists on practicing safe sex.

"My story is a little unconventional. My husband and I are polyamorists, which means that we are dedicated and loyal to each other but we are not monogamous. We are also not swingers; not that there's anything wrong with that, it's just not what we are. We seek playmates outside of our marriage for long-term sexual intimacy based upon friendship. And yet our marriage comes first. Some people have a hard time understanding the concept, but studies show that marriage comes in many forms. It's just that when a marriage is unconventional in some way, people normally just don't discuss it with others. I've lived in the San Francisco Bay Area all my life and was born to left wing parents who remember their participation in "The Summer of Love." In fact, though I was only eight years old at the time, I too remember it. Perhaps this is why I am so open to polyamory.

Some people may not approve, but the fact of the matter is that the Internet has opened up a whole new world for couples such as us. Normally, it's really hard to find like-minded individuals; the Internet makes it much easier. If you walk into a bar – or any other public place – there is no guarantee that there are any people in there searching for whatever it is you are searching for. By posting or answering an ad like this one, I can efficiently attract the kind of people I am seeking. And by using email, I can safely interview and access such people.

I have yet to have a truly bad experience, probably because I am very strict about how I go about things. I proceed with caution. If the man is being pushy, it's a bad sign and I cut things off. I've met a number of men where there was no chemistry or they seemed a little off, but because I was meeting them for the first time for something simple and informal, like coffee or lunch – with the strict warning that under NO condition would I run off to a motel with them – it's no big deal. And I never do. If the chemistry is there, and I think they are safe, then we can later make a date to play some other time. Also, I make sure the lunch/coffee is always "Dutch Treat." I will not let them buy me anything, as I do not want to feel obligated to them in any way. I always meet for the first time in busy, public places in case it becomes obvious that the man is a nasty, scary person. And I make sure to tell them that my husband knows where I am meeting them, and when. (Ironically, when I was single and trying more conventional ways to meet men, I had a number of bad experiences. I met one guy at my church that stalked me for six months!)

Anyway, after the lunch/coffee, I can usually tell if they are interested. If they are not, or there doesn't seem to be any chemistry, I am up-front about it. I'll politely tell them that I don't think that I am their type – and no hard feelings. However, if we are both interested, I will send them my basic sex rules. I want to make sure they understand what my limits are and what I think safe sex is, and also hygiene issues. So far, I have yet to have a negative reaction to my rules. In fact, men tell me that they like me being up-front.

Unfortunately, I have yet to find an "intimate encounters" forum, which where my ad actually belongs. I have been disease free all my life, and I intend to stay that way. Casual encounters are exactly that: casual. And sex is nothing to be casual about. I'm really more interested in long term attachments based on friendship, trust and sex. There's a big difference.

I realize that like all choices in life, we all have to

make our own decisions about how we do or do not behave sexually. I am sure there are plenty of people who have casual encounters that turn out just fine. It's their choice. But there are risks involved. Stalkers, transients looking for someone to take advantage of, STDs, HIV, sadists looking for a convenient victim to beat the crap out of. I know I can't guarantee to myself that I can always avoid such people, but I have decided that the best way to avoid someone HIV+ is to habitually stay away from casual encounters and the people who engage in them. By following this plan of action, I've yet to have a bad experience. That doesn't mean it won't happen some day, but so far so good. **"**

# ???? CAN GAY GO STRAIGHT ????

I have been gay for as long as my memory goes back. Been attracted to nothing but men, but lately, I've noticed I can't stop staring at the beautiful women that walk by. Maybe this phase is over, who knows? I want to experiment with a woman and see if it's what I want. Please send a picture and a brief description of what I would be getting into. Your pic gets mine.

Me: early 20's, 5'11, 180, fit, good looking and love to have fun. Clean as well and would appreciate the same. Hope to hear from you!

" I have had a few responses to this ad and a few others I've posted, but it usually ALWAYS has the same result . . . frustration. Once in a while, people get lucky and have a great experience. Of course those people are mostly women, because we all know that it is so much easier for women to get laid then men. I, of course, have been gay for a long time and recently have been interested in women. The thing is, half of the responses from my ad still come from men. Although I am/was gay, I find that the gay men I see online are all the same with the exception of a few. The responses I received from men were mostly the same too. They'd typically include a picture of their package with something as simple as, "Why would you want to leave that?" How original. Either that, or they send me an email telling me about how they used to be bi and hated sex with women and yada, yada, yada. Of course they are probably just telling me this to get their foot in the door so they can try and get laid with me.

Meanwhile, the women that responded to my ad all fit the same profile. BIG and UGLY. Not to be mean, but that is what they were. When they first sent me emails, I asked for descriptions of what they looked like, and they did not hesitate to make themselves sound like a goddess. I have to admit, some of the stuff that women sent me through emails got me rock hard and I couldn't wait to meet to live it out. But a couple of times when I showed up, I found myself pretending I was never there and turned right around. It was quite disappointing. And of course, lo and behold, within the next couple days of me standing them up, I get the hate email. *"Why didn't you show? I thought you were different!!!"* My response was simple, *"I thought you were different too."*

I have posted another ad wanting to explore a threesome with a man and a woman because I wanted to ease myself into it. Needless to say that all the responses I got were from men. Some claimed that they had girlfriends, and a few of those seemed like they actually might have. But after talking back and forth through emails for a bit, most of them started making excuses of why their girlfriends or friends couldn't make it, 'but that of course shouldn't stop us from meeting and having fun'. One of them claimed that his girl-friend fell and broke her ankle and wouldn't be doing any "activities" for a while. Then he got mad at me when I didn't want to have sex with just him. I mean, I'm gay, but I still say freely that most gays are frickin' hypocritical idiots.

So my conclusion about my online experiences is simple. The women that post are either men that are trying to collect pictures of other men, or, they are fairly large women that don't have too much luck when you base everything on first appearance. But for some reason, I am still uncontrollably drawn to these ads. Sometimes I just like talking dirty through emails and seeing what can happen. It's almost like a fetish.

I've heard some stories that others have said about them hooking up with the perfect woman, but I think most of those were lies to make them feel better about themselves.

One other thing that bugs me is the hypocrisy of women. They are the least bit attractive or in shape. Most of them have an IQ of a bottle of Crisco, but yet, they still require the men that respond to be six feet tall, muscular, extremely sexy and clean cut. Hmmmmm. Does this seem unfair? LOL! That, I would have to say, is the most irritating of all.

Even with all the negatives though, I can't help checking the ads out. I know there are the hot ones out there. They are just few and far between. I have hooked up with a couple of men and had some decent experiences when it came down to it, but they always ended up being drama queens when it was over. I think that most people can be who they aren't here, and that is what screws things up. People expect one thing and get another. That's what pisses people off. So all in all, it's a 'Catch-22.' You hate it, but you love it. I don't get it myself. I just keep going back for more. "

# Got the munchies, don't know what to eat

I'm a 31 yr old female bored with my life looking to add some extra excitement to it. Just hitting my prime sexual peak. I'm ready, waiting and willing to use it!  I'm looking for a relationship with no strings attached, purely sexual pleasures for each of us. I want a person who wants to satisfy the other as well as themselves. Any takers?

" To get to the point, one of my adventures was a long time fantasy come true. I would have to say since the age of about thirteen or fourteen; I have always wanted to have a sexual experience with another female. Anyway, about a month ago now, I met someone online. We arranged a time and place to meet for a drink just to see if we clicked or not. We got along fine and about two hours later I was really doing things I had only ever dreamed of. I fully enjoyed myself, until she became weird. She sat on top of me and wouldn't let me leave. I started getting a little nervous about the whole situation, but she finally let me go with me promising to see her again soon. I feel horrible because I avoid her as much as I can, but it really did turn into a scary situation. I thought that a woman would be harmless. I guess I was wrong. I still want to have more encounters with women though. I'm just a little more cautious now. "

# Looking for Adventure!

I am an eater of mangos and intrepid skier of bunny slopes.
I have scaled cemetery walls at midnight. I have befriended
monkeys in Malaysia and met mountain goats in Montana.
I once saved a pigeon in Paris from assault by a plastic
bag. I have walked inside of Dahli's head in the Costa
Brava. I have fearless laughter. I have consulted the oracle
of Delphi. I have successfully escaped the labyrinths of
The Tube and The Metro. I've had my 15 seconds of fame on a
TV quiz show. I play with fire and run with scissors. I am
an enigma. My dog really did eat my homework. I have braved
Death Valley in the midst of winter. I have navigated the
salt marshes of Les Sables d'Olone in a canoe. I have been
thrown out of a plane twice.

"  This ad listing got me three hours of mind-blowing sex, but then I was promptly blown off. I made a romantic gourmet dinner and lit the candles. He showed up and after two minutes of idle chat my shirt was off. He lifted me up and threw me against the refrigerator and I wrapped my legs around his waist. The door handles were sticking in my back so I whispered that we go upstairs to my bedroom. We barely made it up the stairs. Then it was a sensual exploration of bodies. I don't remember exactly what happened because my mind was a swill of color sensation and I had lost my vocabulary. Three hours later we decided that we had earned dinner. As he left he said that he would call later, but he never did..... "

# Looking for fun and a good lover

I'm a 28 year-old funny, smart, attractive, professional horny woman looking for a man, 28-40, for fun, sex and whatever else. Must like to have fun and explore in bed. I'm looking for someone real, who I can trust and respect. I have brown hair and eyes, a cute smile, round hips, perky tits and no inhibitions. Hope to hear from you soon.

" I used to unashamedly use newspaper personals in the past to meet people for dates. Well, casual sex really. This was back when it was still a fairly new practice and considered seedy by most people. I suppose it still is in a way. But I've always been one to try new things and I guess it was only natural for these types of ads to wind up in electronic format and on the Internet, and for me to give them a try too.

After all . . . why not? It's all right there for your immediate gratification. If you can go grocery shopping online, why not go looking for a hook-up there too? Of course, you do need to be careful, use your instincts and some common sense. But because I'm busy, don't get out much, not all that social to begin with, and perhaps even a little lazy, I do find that this is a great way to have some uncomplicated, casual fun.

My friends think I'm crazy and are worried that I'll end up with a psycho killer or something. Their opinion is that only losers have to go online to meet people. But I've found that most people approach this as not so much of a last resort, but instead take a "let's see if this works" type of approach while trying other things too.

I originally started looking for lust online shortly after moving to Seattle from the U.K. They were much more sexually open over there and not afraid to come right up to you and ask if you 'fancied a shag' outright. Of course, this was usually after a few pints of Courage, but at least they were straightforward and open about it. Here, everyone is afraid to put it out there in a social situation for fear of rejection. Or they've lost interest in sex because they're too caught up working out at the gym, owning their condos or working at their dot-com job. That's messed up.

I'm not a nympho or anything, but *come on!* This girl's got needs and I wasn't getting them fulfilled any time soon here in the Emerald City. So I went looking online for others who might be in the same situation. At least with the Internet, you can split the difference between putting yourself out there and risking rejection. If you *do* get rejected, you haven't really lost any face because you haven't experienced physical rejection in front of someone after seeing you in person for the first time. And you've avoided the awkwardness of that initial first meeting if you don't hit it off right away. It's much easier to initiate a conversation, exchange a few photos and decide then and there if you're attracted to each other or not. If not, there's no harm done.

That said, the Internet doesn't erase the social norms and basic good manners you need in order to interact with others. You do still need to make an effort. I get a lot of responses from my ads that say, "Hey you sound cool. Let's hook up." Sorry guys, but you have to do better than that. I'm not interested in your stats or photos of your penis. You need to have some charm and find some way to stand out from all the rest to hold my attention.

This is different than getting and keeping someone's attention in a bar, for example, or all the other ways single people meet other single people. You can't be as honest about yourself and what you're looking for in a bar. You have to make more effort instead to be physically appealing to the other person so they'll accept you, than to be yourself. You can express yourself and your attitudes and views far better initially with someone over the Internet and get to know them on another level than just the physical one. It's a good way of dipping your toe in the water and frees you up to talk to each other about things other than sex. Physical attraction can be very distracting.

That said, I don't really expect to meet my soul mate online and would be really surprised if I were to meet someone of any real substance within the two dimensions of the Internet. It's too artificial and difficult to make any real connections. And while most people here in the casual encounters area are all looking for the same thing, I still find a lot of guys who really just want to have sex but are too afraid to admit it and getting shot down. We'd all be a lot happier if everyone was just honest and more straightforward about what they want. When people see my ad they know that I'm not looking for a boyfriend, just sex, and they know exactly what I'm looking for. And so boundaries are set and respected right up front, there are no expectations or misunderstandings and no one gets hurt.

I've been placing ads like this one off and on for about three and a half years now, depending on whether I was seeing someone, etc. I've had lots of responses from this particular posting and eventually met up with three people in person. One of which was exactly what I was looking for and turned into a fling, but it didn't last very long (about a month). He was seeing someone else at the time that was turning into more of a regular thing, so we broke things off. I was a little disappointed that it didn't last longer but that's the risk you take with something like this.

I'm pretty selective about who I meet up with and have never slept with anyone that I wasn't at least fond of. But I don't fall in love as easily as I used to and I don't seek the same validation of being in a relationship that I used to. I can totally be in the moment, enjoy myself, remember the boundaries and have sex with someone without having to be in a relationship. I fully expect the men that I'm with to do their own thing and have their own lives outside of mine. All I want from them is some basic trust, respect and honesty. (And a good shag from time to time.) And while I use as much common sense as possible, there's no way to live life and be one hundred percent safe all of the time – sexually, emotionally, etc. While others tend to fall into relationships and limit their number of sexual partners in order to be "safe," I prefer to have lots of partners and use condoms religiously. When you become emotionally involved, for most people condoms tend to go out the window. And I think that's far more risky when you take into account the number of past partners the other person may have had unprotected sex with before meeting you. It would take a *lot* of time and a number of HIV tests before I'd ever be willing to get to that point.

So far I've never had any ugly experiences online, nor have I met anyone who wanted to stalk me or chop me up into tiny pieces. Most of the people I've encountered were very normal, open-minded and equally frustrated with meeting people other ways and/or were interested in expanding their horizons and didn't think that it was weird to want to try different things. I've been able to experiment in ways that I normally wouldn't be able to, and approach people, in other circumstances. There's no other way I could make this happen and I certainly wouldn't approach any of my friends about this.

Overall I've met up with about a dozen or so people this way (including a few couples who were looking for someone to have a threesome with). I've also cybered with people and have had phone sex numerous times. It's certainly not the same as being with someone in person, but it does scratch an itch and satisfies an immediate need in the moment, especially when you know you're not going to be meeting that particular person for actual sex any time soon.

So I guess I'll continue at this until I do meet that psycho killer, get burned emotionally, become involved in a more serious relationship or simply outgrow it. But it's not for everyone. You need to know yourself pretty well and trust your instincts when meeting people this way and be prepared for anything to happen. And don't expect to necessarily meet that special some-one through the personal ads – they're not out there. Just a lot of horny people. 🙶

# Here for you, as much as me

I like people! I am interested in finding mature couples for an ongoing adult relationship. Age and shape not a boundary. (But I do have my preferences.) Need a couple that desires starting off slow and letting it grow - testing the limitations of our fantasies. You must be open minded and willing to try, because that is why I am here! I want normal people who like nudity, the outdoors, fun sex, and nice conversation. I just want simple uncomplicated people to kick back, have fun, and enjoy the company. You need to be respectful of others, honest, and take pride in your appearance. I will be glad to return the same personal respect! If you have a preconceived notion of single guys, then I can break it for you. I am not here to just have sex and go. Would thoroughly enjoy a long-term situation with one or more couples. I would enjoy quiet adult evenings, good food, and quality fun for everyone. If you don't think this is possible, contact me and we will conquer the stereotypes. I am here for you, as much as me. TAKE A CHANCE. Discretion, privacy, and respect are on top of my list. I hope they are on yours too.

" I am a thirty-two year old male living in Florida and have been an active participant in the swinging alternative lifestyle for some time now. I am well traveled, both in the States as well as abroad. I come from a great family where my parents are still married and we are all self-supportive and positive people. One day in high school, as I was driving home I noticed a magazine in the road and stopped to check it out. Lo and behold it was a swingers magazine. Up until that point I had no idea or even considered that this was a feasible lifestyle. But oh was I intrigued. I did not submit or respond to any of the ads and just moved on with normal daily life but it never left me. I was intrigued about the couples seeking couples, men seeking women, women seeking women, and every imaginable offer to meet strangers for sex.

I had been approached while in high school a few times by men and always adamantly turned them down. It was not until college that I allowed another man to orally satisfy me. Then came the mixed feelings. "Am I gay, weird, confused, experimenting . . . what was the meaning of this?" But I was damn sure of one thing – it felt great! It was fun, and it was a turn on. And as long as nobody would find out, I knew right then I would do it again. So while I maintained relationships and dated girls steadily for long periods of time, I decided that it was time to pursue the alternative lifestyle.

I went to the Post Office (this was pre 9/11) and opened a fictitious Post Office Box, wrote my personals ad for a swingers magazine, paid my $20, sent it in and waited for all the responses to come rolling in. To my utter amazement it didn't happen like I wanted. I got a few responses from some great couples and I got a plethora of responses from men. Single men, married men, divorced men, short men, fat men, hairy men, dads, coaches, CEO's . . . all walks and ways of life. I was astounded, and realized that the swinging market is full of men! The over abundance would have frogs changing sexes, so to speak, to accommodate for the out-of-balance in the swinging community. I noticed that snail mail was getting more expensive than ever, and the average turnaround time on each letter sent was about two weeks. I figured by the time I actually met any of these people it could be six months down the road. Eventually, I did meet up with a few people (men), and started letting some of them take care of me. Selfishly, I was not reciprocating because I was not gay, but I did want to have some accomplishments with my personal ad. And damn it, like I said before, it felt gooooood!

Then came the Internet and all it joyous privacy. I could be who I am or not. I could ask questions, tell stories and experiment with all kinds of people online. I was starting to understand and come to terms with who I was and what I wanted. It was very clear to me that I enjoyed women, first and foremost. But I had occurrences with men and enjoyed those too. I had to ask myself what it was that I was looking for, ultimately.

Then it dawned on me to put my focus towards couples. I could have women while their men were nearby. And maybe, if I were lucky, they would be like the married guys on the Internet and have the same curiosities. I was wrong. All the couples placing ads were looking for straight men. I could not bear to put myself in a situation where I could not have both, because I knew I enjoyed both. I came home one day and typed "swingers" into a search engine and WHAM! Swingers on the Internet! I couldn't believe it. (These days, of course, it's a lot more commonplace.)

I placed my first online swingers ad on a site approximately three months ago and it has been wonderful. I met with a great couple, and after corresponding and learning about each other's wants and desires it was the most sensual experience. I have met with some men, a few women and am presently getting ready to meet with another couple.

Online dating has been a pleasure because it is instantaneous — you can meet and learn about what qualifies you or them to be candidates to service each other's needs. You get to see them by exchanging photos to find out if there's a physical attraction, chat with them to find mutual ground, and best of all, everybody knows why you are talking. It is not misconstrued when some-one or everyone is interested in a common goal. Sex. Simply find an ad that strikes you, send a reply, talk about it and then make an educated decision.

What this all has taught me and what I have come to realize, is that not only is there an abundance of wonderful sexual experiences available to you, but that others think just like you, act like you, have fantasies and desires like you, and want to share them and express them with others.

I am also finding more couples interested in single men and learning that labels are not part of my existence. I am not "gay" because I have had sex with men. Nor am I "straight" because I have had sex with women. And I am definitely not "bi" because I have had sex with both and enjoyed it.

I am just me. I am Larry. I am a man that enjoys companionship as well as sex – sex without labels. In my mind, people are supposed to enjoy each other, and for the most part we do. We enjoy humans socially – singularly as well as in groups. So why is it so uncharacteristic, or deemed "wrong," that we should not enjoy each other in the same compassionate manner, sensually?

We all have desires, fantasies, and curiosities, and I believe we only limit our human abilities by hiding behind labels, society's stigmatism, and our judgmental and repressive education and support system that we actually make people feel shame for fear of being judged by others.

In my life I have extinguished labels and am very comfortable in the fact that I am a very honest person who enjoys people – all people – for their compassion, general belief in humanity and their sensuality. I refuse to bury my emotions on the fact that sexually I enjoy the company of women as equally as that of men. Simply put, I consider myself lucky to be able to enjoy all of God's creatures without guilt or judgment. This is because I am the only one with the authority to judge my own emotions and feelings. I just wish more people were so lucky. ,,

# Doc looking for fun

I used to be the quiet, shy type. Now I want to explore my wild side. I want a man who can be both a friend and a passionate lover...someone who can excite me with just a look, a word, or a simple touch.

" I am engaged to a man that I met two years ago through an online dating service. Both of us are now on this personals site for fun but we're not looking for actual meetings with people in real life. We enjoy erotic chatting and emails with others we meet from the personals. It ends up spicing up our relationship in and out of the bedroom. We're not looking to cheat on each other, have an open relationship and invite others in or anything like that – just fantasy role-playing sort of stuff.

I discovered online dating about six years ago. I was working a lot in the medical profession (still do) and found it very difficult to work a long day and then try to go out and meet new people at night. I was just too pooped. I started playing this trivia game that I found online by accident one evening and wound up spending hours at a time playing it somewhat frequently. One day I started to join in on the chatting sessions going on between games and even during the games themselves. It was a lot of fun.

I found that I could cut loose online and be as funny or obnoxious or even as quiet as I wanted to be without feeling like I had to be a certain way. I eventually started encountering people online who wanted to have cyber-sex. I was pretty shy about the whole thing at first but thought I'd give it a try.

I didn't participate much the first few times, but only read what my cyber partner was sending to me. They were cool with that and knew I would catch on when I was ready. Boy did I ever! It seemed to come very naturally for me to write about the things that I was fantasizing about, and before I knew it, I was hooked. I even developed a little cyber strip tease for the people I'd be chatting with. I would describe exactly what I was wearing and what I was taking off . . . it would get pretty hot. Even some of the women in the chat rooms would send me private messages wanting to cyber!

At the time that I was learning about cybering, I was still a virgin. I watched porn, read erotic stories and, of course, read all of the sex tips in Cosmopolitan so that I would know what to do when the right time came. Cybering with people allowed me to try out some of the things that I had learned, albeit through the use of words rather than acting them out in person.

I guess the other overall appeal of chatting online is that you can remain anonymous if you choose. You don't have to worry about someone finding out that you are kinky or a prude, or that you will embarrass yourself. It doesn't have to matter online. It is NOT real life. Of course, if you do hit it off with someone through the Internet, you can choose to take it to the next level. It's all up to you. That is what I did almost five years ago now. I met someone online and we quickly became friends. We chatted constantly and eventually met in person and dated when we could, but we lived very far apart. So in between visits, we did a lot of cybering together. When you're 2,500 miles apart and can only see each other in person two or three times a year, you need to do something! I looked at it as the modern day love letter . . . full of sex! Ultimately though, that relationship ran its course and came to an end as our ages, and life and family goals were just too different.

That's when I decided to give Internet dating a try. I found this dating site that looked pretty easy and so I filled out a profile with my likes and dislikes, included some photos and any other personal information that I wanted people to know and put up the dough for a three-month membership.

I was immediately overwhelmed with messages all at the same time. It was freaky! That first day there had to be at least twenty guys paging me to chat with them.

Meeting the men online and getting so much attention made me feel good about myself again. The breakup with my ex really destroyed my self-esteem, but the attention from these people helped to rebuild it. My fiancé was actually the very first person to contact me on that site.

We chatted back and forth for a few weeks before I agreed to a date. (He was also the first one I agreed to meet with in person.) He traveled over two hundred miles to see me. I was extremely impressed and had a great time. Of course, I took him by my office to let my coworkers meet him. They wanted to make sure that they could identify him if I ever turned up missing . . . LOL!

I was very up-front and honest with him. I didn't want to be in a relationship yet and he was fine with that. He was so cute when he said goodbye after the date. He said that I would be in love with him in six months, but that he would wait for me forever if necessary.

I had a few other dates since then that were fun, but no sparks like with my fiancé.

I did have one rather bad experience with a fireman from a neighboring town. He started right off with a rude comment when he came to pick me up. He wanted to know where a good place to have lunch would be. I asked him what he was in the mood for and he said, "Hair pie." I could have smacked him! The lunch date went downhill after that.

He was in the middle of a nasty divorce and kept talking about his ex. He never missed a chance to let me know that he wanted to get into my pants. He tried more than once to cop a feel of my boobs when we were walking to the car. He was a dog and the one date I didn't take to my co-workers for approval. I guess that can be advice to anyone who is going to date someone from the Internet – have friends and family check them out!

My fiancé and I eventually started to see more of each other and before I knew it, I had fallen for him. It snuck right up on me as he predicted, and hit me when I was driving over to spend the holidays with him and his family.

Since all of my family is over two thousand miles away, it was great to have someone to spend the holidays with again. I was, and am, completely smitten and we're getting married next April.

# I'm sad and feeling lonely

I don't know what I'm looking for and I don't even know if I'm looking for something or someone... Maybe I just want a friend... I DON'T KNOW... I don't want to get hurt again... and I DON'T WANT A RELATIONSHIP... NO MORE COMMITMENTS!

" I started using the Internet to meet people the first time I moved to the United States back in 2001. In the beginning it was out of curiosity, plus I had a lot of free time on my hands. I was looking for companions because I was tired of the bar scene. These days, if I go to a club now it is just to have a drink and to dance (sometimes just by myself). With the Internet I can filter who I want to talk to, or not talk to, unlike in a nightclub because sometimes men don't respect you or your decisions. If you say "no" they often continue to insist and bother you. So for me, it's a lot easier to meet people who I find interesting, attractive and compatible this way.

This particular experience was rather sad for me though. I posted this ad one day when I was feeling quite sad and lonely after a brief love affair had ended and I found myself alone again.

Everything started out like a game. I met a guy who was visiting from Miami through this website and we got pretty involved. I didn't intend to get so intimate with him as I was engaged at the time, but my fiancé travels a lot for his work and so I find myself home and alone much of the time. I HATE to be alone. I'm a very sexual, sensual person and I need to be touched and to feel loved constantly. My fiancé and I are very compatible sexually and he satisfies me completely . . . when he is home. When he is not, you can only take matters into your own hands for so long. ;-)

After meeting this man and conversing over email we decided to talk on the phone and made arrangements to meet a couple of days later. I asked him if he would like to join my daughter and I for dinner, thinking that he would say no. But he went anyway. When we arrived, I saw someone waiting outside thinking that it might have been him.

He was much larger than how he looked in his photo (I only saw his face) so I started hiding myself, not sure if I should approach him or not.

I was cautious because this has happened to me before in the past. The Internet makes it easy for people to misrepresent themselves or become something they are actually not, and so you have to be careful. One time, back when I was living in New York, I met a Mexican man online. I fell into his game. I was very stupid. I believed his story of having broken up with his girlfriend and fucked him for a while. Three months later his girlfriend was back in town and he said he wanted to give her another try, and so he got back together with her again. I felt very used

Another New York man posted a very nice picture of himself with his ad. He was very handsome and athletic and everything. I meet him and he was like 100 pounds overweight and balding. That was awful! His photo was either altered or it wasn't actually him.

So I was nervous when I saw this man waiting outside of the restaurant. But it wasn't him. Ten minutes later he arrived and I recognized him as the man I was actually waiting for, and in person he was so much more than what I was expecting. There was instant chemistry. He was very tall, had an athletic build, beautiful blue eyes, was really handsome and we had so many things in common. We were even born on the same day. The best part was that he got along great with my daughter during the dinner.

Afterwards we went to my house together and I poured us some wine. After about our third glass we were sitting close together and he told me he was shy. I told him that I was the same and that I was not going to kiss him. So he asked if I would refuse him if he tried to kiss me. I said "no" and so he did. Thirty minutes later we were in my bed. After that we didn't part for ten days.

We were like a perfect match together and he made me feel so special – kissing me all the time, not letting our bodies get apart (not even for a second), telling me I was incredible and beautiful, hugging me all of the time . . . everything. It was pure passion. He was not just fucking me.

It started out casual but turned into something more for both of us. A few days later he told me that he loved me, and the next weekend we went out together and he asked me to marry him. I said no, because I was already engaged . . . plus we were a little drunk. And he was leaving town in a couple of days and I was not going to run away with someone I just met ten days ago.

After he left, I had the distinct impression that he would've tried to take advantage of me (financially). He did not have a job where he was going and he was trying to get me to sell the house before I broke it off.

Plus, after a while he changed his mind and said he didn't want to marry me anymore and wanted to just live together and then see what would happen. I eventually broke it off and he left. We parted on good terms and remained in contact for a while, but eventually we stopped communicating.

I was feeling sad one day afterwards because I felt we really got to love each other, but it would not have worked. I placed this ad because I was lonely and I didn't want to be alone. I wanted a friend . . . with benefits, but not a lover. I had many responses, but so far nothing has happened.

I haven't met anyone yet that I find interesting and attractive enough to meet. But since I am getting married soon I will probably remove the ad, as I don't want to screw things up with him. I think I just need to feel wanted and needed, and to have the nice feeling of loving someone – a partner – more than just a friend.

I really shouldn't be alone. I'm not the kind of woman who can be alone. I HATE BEING ALONE. But I'll be married soon and my husband should be here with me all the time – at least every night – and I won't have to turn to the Internet for love and affection. 99

# New in the area, looking for a little fun...

I am a reasonably good-looking, professional, middle-aged, masculine/straight acting Bi-male. Here's what I am looking for.... guys who enjoy being kissed and touched all over. You need to be clean and disease free, (duh). I don't like prophylactics. I own my own home with a pool and have a private place to play. Plus, I don't really care for pushy or obnoxious guys. Be respectful and not into pain. You must be willing to lay back and enjoy like never before — the ultimate would be all night! Body types and sizes are not as important as the clean and disease free part! I live in Las Vegas, but travel to major business areas from time to time. I am only looking for 1 or 2 discrete guys to play with on a regular basis. One more thing... if you're a "straight-8" curious guy, and just want one "walk-on-the-wild side" to kind of see what it's like -- please get in touch with me. I love to take straight-8s to the highest level. (You might have heard that before - LOL!) But seriously, the initial pleasure is just the beginning. The beginning of an "all night" you will never forget!

❝ I had my first same sex experiences when I was a kid with an older guy, and loved it. Next was my college roommate; we'd help each other out whenever we couldn't get a date. Then, a curious hot young guy I met at a 24-hour health club; we'd sneak into the weight room late at night. Finally, a married guy I met at a business conference. We went out for a couple of drinks after the last meeting and ended up back at his hotel room. I couldn't believe how excited I was. He "enjoyed" himself not two feet away from me and I blushed a deep crimson red. He then asked if I was going to join him. I paused for a moment, and then, did. We had an extremely enjoyable evening. As wacky as it may sound, I loved the fact that he was married – I've never enjoyed it more. Even more interesting is the fact that I enjoyed being his sexual servant. We've since become "conference-buddies" and meet up occasionally when we can.

Needless to say, I'm a very sexual person. I'm genuinely poly-erotic and enjoy both sexes, and all age groups. I've been using the Internet to meet people for my sexcapades since 1997. To me, it's a great way to meet like-minded, sexy people. I'm fascinated with people, and I thought it was more honest than going to bars. I also find it somewhat erotic. People will tell you the most interesting, intimate things when they're online – things they probably wouldn't say in a bar or other venue.

To date, I've met up with over fifty people this way ranging from single, married, and divorced of both sexes. I met one lady who was having sex with her son. (We had a few incredible three-ways.)

I was invited to a private (invitation only) sex club one time. I think that was the most erotic thing I've ever done. Not only was there an incredible show on stage, people (of both sexes) were "performing" at almost every angle; but the couple who invited me, both sucked me during the show. It may sound fantastic, but believe me, we were mild compared to what others were doing.

I guess my personal favorite is women (wives, really) who want to watch their husband suck another guy off. I like the eroticism of the whole scene, I especially like to screw the wife, and watch the husband's reaction while I'm doing it. I like it even better when I coax him into going down on her afterwards.

Another favorite is the younger (adult) guys who are practically walking hard-ons. They are actually in pain from the "blue-nuts" syndrome. One, in particular, calls me late at night pretty frequently when his date didn't go as planned. He just wants to come by for a quick blowjob. More than once he's brought a few of his buds with him and I've sucked them all off (a couple of times the same night). Then, as easy as you please, we all shake hands, they thank me, and they leave.

Another is just your typical computer nerd. When I first met him online, he had never had sex at all. He finally agreed to come over and we started watching a little porn. I didn't tell him what I was going to do, and all of a sudden, I pulled it out and started gently masturbating. He didn't say one word about what I was doing and just continued to stare at the action on the screen.

As I got more into it, I got up, stood in front of him and pulled him forward. Strangely enough, when I was through, I slumped back down beside him and he never said a thing, just kept watching the video. We did that several times. When we finished the second movie, we bade our goodbyes and he left. He still calls me up from time to time, and asks if he can come over.

My absolute favorite is straight guys. I love to seduce them with my writing skills, over the computer, and then verbally over the phone. Once I get them going a little, they come to my place "at least for a handjob." When they get here, I almost always talk them into letting me screw them before they leave.

Admittedly, most have to get a little drunk first, but they all secretly know they want to be seduced. One guy, in particular, is super. He comes to see me regularly, but I have to "seduce" him (according to him, against his will) every time. Which, quite frankly, is a turn-on for me.

Lastly, I met this older lady, in her seventies. I thought it would be kinky to see what she'd be up for. So, we visited on the computer for quite some time – several months, actually. She kept telling me I was being silly, and I kept talking (typing) "dirty" to her, telling her what nasty little things I'd like to do to her when we meet up.

I finally got her to come over to my house and when she got here, I had another of my male friends from out of town with me. Believe it or not, we started watching a little porn, with her between us. It wasn't long before I unzipped and pulled my dick out.

She too didn't say anything initially, and kept watching the movie. So eventually, after I got into it a little more I stood up and got in front of her like I do with my nerd friend, and started stroking myself inches from her face. That got her attention. She started taking care of me immediately. I told my bud  to take his cock out, and she gave us both very enthusiastic blowjobs. It was amazing! Then, we moved into the bedroom did a very kinky three-way with her. Believe me, it was too, too much.

I've never had the least bit of a bad experience from my Internet encounters. Like most of life, one can find trouble when one goes looking for it, but . . . my personal experiences were honest, graceful, very wholesome (in that both parties knew up-front what they wanted to do and the limits respected), and disease free.

I'm still moseying around on the web looking for new people to play with. Maybe I'm just the proverbial "dirty old man," who knows?

I'll say this though. If I am, there are a lot of people like me online and off. Also, everyone always said they enjoyed what we did, and most came back for more. "

# suddenly solo in orlando

I'm a hot, sexy, curvaceous, 36 y/o party girl with trouble in mind. My companion is stuck in the northeast due to bad weather delays, so I'll be arriving in Orlando tomorrow (Sunday) all by myself. Seeking NSA encounter, maybe dinner first? Send a picture and I'll be glad to reciprocate.

My husband and I don't talk anymore. I can't look him in the eye. Every time I ask him a question, he responds with a question. I say, "Do you need anything at the store?" And he responds, "*Do* I need anything at the store?" So I've stopped asking him anything at all. Instead, I have learned to talk with other men. At first, I didn't feel like I was officially cheating, because I didn't sleep with any of them. Then I found out about online classifieds ads. There are all kinds of postings, absolutely free, for every kind of desire. (There's also a lot of exercise equipment for sale as well.)

I started to post messages, but never with my real name. Here's how I worked it out: I wasn't cheating on my husband because I wasn't having actual sex. My love life was divided into three parts: the men I dated but did not bed, the men I had virtual sex with but did not meet, and the man I married.

I found myself checking the postings every night. Guys would send me messages and I would rarely respond unless I read something distinguished. I ruled out almost all of them. Then there was Brad. Something about the tone of his email messages intrigued me. After we exchanged a dozen emails, he gave me his cell phone number. Turns out we grew up blocks from one another. Several years ago, I was looking for a house. The realtor showed me a town house next to a synagogue. I discovered that was Brad's parents' house. I had unknowingly walked through the dining room he'd eaten in, up the stairs he used a thousand times, and into his childhood bedroom. It was like that between Brad and I. He played a musical instrument, designed buildings, and had a history of doing drugs. Now he was driving a BMW, buying raw loft space, and attending AA meetings, even on Christmas. And he was kinky.

Brad wanted to spank me in the worst way. He wanted nothing more than to put me over his knee. Our conversations concerned him pulling my hair, shaving me, handing me a mirror so I could watch. This was simultaneously intriguing and extremely frightening. I liked it as a phone sex concept, but was appalled by the idea of actually submitting to that kind of treatment.

It turned out that Brad and I had many people in common. I would not tell him my real name or where I worked. But he told me everything. My silence, my withholding, was my only power.

He would call me in the middle of the day and I would realize he was driving on a road I'd driven only hours before. We could have met a dozen times at the market, or the record store. He had an email address for me, one that I had made up specifically for corresponding with him. He'd send me poetry, or alternatively, call me a dog. I grew to love talking to him. He turned me on. And then afterwards, we'd talk for hours about everything else. He even called me from a toy store once to ask my advice on what to buy for his niece. He became my voice boyfriend. I had no idea what he looked like, and he only had a mental picture of me.

He begged me to meet him. Anywhere. He was increasingly desperate. But I could not do it. Maybe it was the threat of spanking. Maybe it was the threat of disappointing him with my human form. Online I am perfectly proportioned, endlessly sexy, a bomb waiting to explode. In real life I have big blue eyes, sexy tits and a party attitude. I am also an exhausted, over-weight, moody mom.

All this was taking place in the weeks leading up to New Year's Eve. We talked several times a day.

He would give me possible scenarios for meeting. He promised me our affair would remain a secret. He knew that I was dating other men, actually meeting them in restaurants, and driving around in their cars, so he couldn't figure out why I would not date him.

His anger turned self-righteous. His ex-junkie self would come down hard on me, accusing me of unethical behavior in my marriage. He was beginning to wonder why he was interested in me, given that I had some real issues with honesty. But still he pleaded with me to cross that line with him.

I agreed to meet Brad on the last day of the year, to finally have our first date. I managed to get my husband and kids out of the house for the night. It was 8:30 pm, December 31st. I stalled, and eventually chickened out. I would not leave my house and I would not tell him where I lived. At 10:00 I was firmly planted on my couch, watching television, and getting stoned. Then at 11:42 I called to tell him I loved him. In the background there was the typical raucous NYE party noise, screaming, loud music, etc. I called him again at 11:58, just before all circuits became busy. That was the last conversation we ever had.

I tried to call him many times afterwards, but he would not answer. I would leave seductive messages on his voice mail. But it was over for him. He'd gotten fed up. I realized that he was right. I was not being honest with my husband, and it was time to ask for a divorce. I took him out for coffee and told him it was time for us to separate. I could not tell him about Brad and the lying, about all the other men I was dating. I only said, "I don't love you the way I should." My husband was totally shocked. He plunged into a depression. He slept, if at all, on the couch. A month passed, then two, then three. But he did not move out. I would remind him that my feelings had not changed. Six months passed and he was still in the house. Eventually he returned to the bed.

Then it was early July. While waiting for a train, a man and I stared each other down on the platform. Hungry, and turned on, I got on the same train car as him and we sat across from one another. What was I thinking? I was on my way to pick up my kids and my stop was next. I got up and never saw him again.

But the encounter was like an electric current. I was fed up with my husband's behavior, and fed up with dating guys and not sleeping with them.

I ended up home alone late one night soon afterwards. My husband and kids were away. I checked the ad postings at 1:00 am, and within a few minutes, I found the right mix of artsy, sexy and local. His name was Michael. *"Who's looking to talk and possibly meet?"* After a few quick emails, a brief exchange over the phone, and a public meeting at the parking lot of the local convenience store, he was in my house. He offered me a cigarette and then asked if he could kiss me. He was a skinny, short person. Delicate even. Tiny, except for one crucial part. I could not believe my good luck.

We went upstairs and did what you would expect. The kinds of things you might read about online. When we finished, I said, "So what's your last name, Michael?" He said, "Actually, my name's not Michael." We got dressed and returned downstairs. It was 3:30 am, and he was on his way out the door. The stench of my bad marriage, like a decaying corpse, had driven me online and ultimately over the line. I called him once, two days later, and left a message. But I never called him again. And I have not heard from him either. Now I think about the wart on his cheek, or the way he smiled when it was all over. A three-quarters smile with something held back. That was the end, right there. But I didn't know it at the time. It had been the real life equivalent of online cyber sex. ,,

# A hard man is good to find.

So, I am going to be in St. Louis for a couple of days, the 4th and 5th, and would like to meet someone in my age range (I'm 39), plus or minus 5 years. I am cute, can mind my manners when I am supposed to, take charge when appropriate or simply go with the flow. I have an athletic body and I have a bit of an edge. Let's start with dinner and no expectations and see where things go. Pic 4 pic. Hope to hear from you soon.

" I generally feel that casual encounters ads are a shout into the void, unless you are female. I talked to one woman recently online who had 300 responses to one ad. My particular post was one of three that I wrote thinking I would try to get laid while in St. Louis (not exactly a hot bed of sexually liberated women). It netted exactly one response – from a guy writing a book.

I've run other m4w ads with moderate success. I am funny, can write to a point of pressing boundaries (without the reader feeling like they are reading a very angry person's wish list), and I feel that it's important to write something that doesn't sound like all the rest of the lonely and lost. The responses generally leave me feeling that the decline of civilization is closer at hand than the next *Garfield* sequel. "

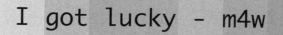

# I got lucky - m4w

I got lucky at Foxwoods and now I have a few extra bucks
to help put a young female through college...
or even a young housewife with some bills. To put it
more bluntly, I have $400 for a non-pro who enjoys
passionate kissing and some fun sex. Daytime is best
for me. What about you?

" I'm an older man so I tried putting out an ad looking for a younger woman. Make no mistake — its all about sex and money — and I understand that perfectly. I don't expect a young woman to meet up with an older man without some compensation. And I always look for the non-pro type, if you will. The student, the housewife and even the career woman. I've met them all and I've slept with them all.

I met this one woman a while back in a 40's chat room and began a lengthy conversation with her. We were both married and not too happy about it. Soon the chat room IMing turned to talking on the phone. I would call her every day and we would talk and talk and talk. She lived on the west coast and I live on the east coast. After talking for about three months we decided that somehow we had to meet. We formulated a plan that we would both bring our spouses to Las Vegas with us and then, while our spouses were busy playing slots or something, we would rendezvous. Now mind you, we've never so much as seen a picture of each other. It wasn't hard to talk our spouses into going to Vegas so that part was easy. We agreed upon a hotel and we described ourselves to the other and set up a meeting at midnight in the lobby where we were staying. I was waiting in the lobby at 11:45 and it was crowded. I scanned the crowd looking for a blonde who would be wearing a skirt. Soon the crowd thinned out and I notice a blonde, in a skirt, standing by herself. I was hesitant and wasn't sure if it was her, so I walked by a few times hoping she would say something to me. She didn't. Finally I got up my courage and approached her and asked, "Are you Marilyn?" She smiled and said, "And you are Tim?" We laughed and talked, and, as we had planned, got our own room. So I had a room with my wife, Marilyn had a room with her husband, and we had our own room that we used three times every day for the next three days. Our spouses never suspected a thing and never knew about it. It was the best weekend of my life. Marilyn was a middle-aged beauty and was personable and incredible in bed. I met her once more, about a year later. I flew out to the west coast on some pretense and we spent another incredible weekend together in a hotel room. We vowed to meet again, but time passed by and 3,000 miles is just too far to maintain a good relationship. I will never forget Marilyn and I know she will never forget me either. 99

# Gentleman interested in safe mutual masturbation.

Greetings,

I am a very fit, educated, unhappily married man, 40 yrs old, clean, d/d free, attractive, full head of hair, totally discreet and safe. I am in town for a few days and would love to have a safe, erotic encounter. Perhaps masturbating in front of each other - without touching. I am interested in getting together with an educated, clean woman who is also in need of some eroticism in a very safe way. Looking forward to one good response.

66 I am a very responsible, happily married, educated, conservative man with two children, but this whole Internet thing has become an incredible obsession. I can easily spend up to six hours a day online and have become addicted to meeting people through email. I've done this quite a bit now and no one would ever know, or even have a clue, about this other side of my life.

I found out about the personal ads while traveling on business one time with some associates. I was instantly hooked and now I go online about three times a day. I don't always go looking to meet up with someone every time, but when I do I am always very, very safe. I usually go with "professionals" but never have any actual inter-course. I've had some bbbj's, but never any vaginal contact. It seems less like cheating that way, especially if I'm paying someone to be with me.

So here's what typically happens. As soon as I check into a hotel room, I immediately search the local papers for massage, escorts, adult services, etc., and then go online to look at the local personals. I usually respond to other people's ads, but the few times that I have posted an ad like this one, I've had ladies contact me and it was not great. Women always, always, always sound and look better in photos than they do in person. But there is something about meeting someone new, having them give me a massage, getting naked and giving me a handjob while looking in my eyes that is so alluring.

My wife has no idea, and as much as I want to be honest, I can't tell her. She would swear that I would never do such a thing. I remain a gentleman in my life – even if I flirt with business associates, I never, ever give off the impression that I would act on it. I feel like I lead a double life. One week I went to four different women (escorts) at about $150 each – which is crazy – and each time I leave I tell myself that I won't go back. But the next day I always feel differently.

All together I have seen about 500 women in the past twelve years. It is staggering how I need to spend $150 for a handjob. My wife is beautiful and we have a wonderful sex life. I often wonder if there are other men out there like me. I feel so driven to search out yet another woman I don't know, to see her breasts for the first time, to have her stimulate me. To have that feeling I love when I'm walking up to her door – that butterfly feeling in my stomach – is like a drug and I can't get enough of it. ""

# want to surprise wife with erotic massage but need practice

I've been taking massage lessons from a friend, so that I can surprise my wife with an expert, erotic massage. But now I need a willing female to practice on. My teacher says I'm very good, but I'm not too confident in my skills yet. Please help me, and get a nice massage too.

66 This ad was posted from a genuine desire to gain skills in erotic massage and to use those skills with my wife. I've taken a few Tantra lessons but I was not too certain about how to actually apply what I've learned. But I have to admit that the prospect of trying out the techniques on women I didn't know was also part of the appeal. As a result of my posts I've met up with a middle-aged woman who was looking for a one-night erotic thrill, a couple (he wanted to watch me massage her, then have sex with her with me watching them) and an Asian woman who wanted me to help her learn how to have an orgasm without using a vibrator. (After about the fourth or fifth time I met with her, she reported that I had helped her with her problem and she'd been successful making herself come with her hands alone. She's now pregnant and engaged to her childhood sweetheart).

I managed to take techniques home that I learned in my massage encounters with people I met through my on-line ads. But I was able to use them in the context of sexual encounters with my wife more than in the context of a massage-only experience. It's more difficult, in many ways, to set aside time and mental space for a massage "appointment" at home – we both assume consciously or unconsciously that if at least one of us is naked and being stroked, it is about sex or it will end in sex, rather than strictly massage or even an erotic massage. So far, when I have used techniques that I've tried out in the massage appointments as part of lovemaking, my wife has been very appreciative. But if we try to replicate the massage experience at home (erotic or not), too many things get in the way. Sex (I mean intercourse) is a goal rather than sensuality per se. The phone rings. The cat starts getting vocal. The one getting the massage, as she peers out the face-hole in the massage table, notices that the floor needs vacuuming. The mental space of marriage is a complete and total package, and it's hard to focus for 60-90 minutes on the one sensual experience of the moment. With a massage appointment, we're strangers, or in the case of repeated appointments, we know each other only through the massage experiences. She can focus on the sensation, and I can focus on giving it. It may be inevitable that the kind of focus on the sensuality of the moment, in the massage itself, is only possible during a massage appointment – a moment between strangers when both parties are focused on strictly that, and not sex. So the experiences based on the online ads will remain, as far as I can tell, unique and not repeatable at home. Whether I'll keep making online massage appointments for themselves, for the experience they uniquely offer regardless of continuing to take home things I learn there, I don't really know. 🙾

# Sex with a stranger....m4w

Have you ever had the desire to meet someone of the opposite
sex for the sole purpose of having sex?
No names.... no commitments.... no strings.... Email me if you
are interested....

66 Much to my shock and surprise I actually got an answer. She claimed to be a female in her 30's and would meet me that very night at a motel somewhere between where she lived and where I lived. I really had my doubts about her, but since the motel we agreed upon wasn't too far from me, I decided to take a chance and see if she would actually show up. She had described her car, as I did mine. At the appointed hour I drove into the parking lot of the motel. There at the end of the lot was the car I was looking for, with a woman, in her 30's looking out the window, searching for me. I drove up to her, confirmed who she was, and got a room. With very little conversation we had uninhibited sex. It was almost weird, but being a man, I was grateful. We never met again or have e-mailed since then because that's how she wanted it to be. She wanted the same thing as me – sex with a stranger – and we both got it. 99

# A burrito and a vibrator.

Let's grab a burrito and then go browse Good Vibes.
We will laugh and try to embarrass one another. Perhaps
we will wander over to the Castro and play with toys in some
of the stores there. Who couldn't use another rubber fist? Or a
gallon of Astro Lube?

Here is what I did this weekend, (this should give you a sense
of me): watched a documentary on I.M. Pei, gessoed wood panels
for drawing and painting, stocked up at Trader Joe's, purchased
new sheets at Bed Bath & Beyond, relaxed at Borders with a
pile of magazines, mocked up a drawing for my new tattoo,
enjoyed the open art studios at Hunters Point Shipyard, and
enjoyed a sushi dinner.

What do you think? Want to wrestle with a big two-headed rubber
dildo?

66 This post introduced me to the craziest, as in insane, woman I've met on the Internet yet.

When she responded to my ad, she told me she was in her mid thirties, but claimed that she looked like she was in her twenties, that she was from a well-off family, highly educated, and a great catch. What I found was a woman that looked well into her forties, pushing 50-something. After talking to her, she disclosed that her family was well off but they had blocked her from getting any of her money, so she received an allowance for living expenses. She never proved in her actions that she had any sort of education, or that she was a "great catch" – not even close. I don't think she even had a job.

Before meeting, she called me constantly at all hours until I agreed to meet her. When I told her I would drive out to her place, she asked if I could stop by a gas station and pick her up some items (gum and Gatorade; she was very particular to which kind) and she told me to bring condoms. Although she did state that this didn't necessarily mean that we would be having sex, (even though she mentioned how horny she had been lately), being the gentleman that I am, I did as she asked.

Once I arrived to her place, a mid-70's apartment complex, I found her unit, which was towards the back. Upon entering I knew this lady was not all she said. For starters, her apartment was decorated like she had purchased everything at a truck stop or a Walgreens. She had cheap furniture, dream catchers, themed throw blankets – it was basically decorated like a white trash home/trailer on *COPS*.

She also, like I mentioned earlier, was a lot older looking than she led on. Like how people that smoke a lot get older-looking more quickly then everyone else. She was a tiny woman, maybe 5'2" or so, and weighed no more than 110. On many women this might look attractive, but she was really thin. She had long stringy dirty blond hair and not the best teeth. When she opened the door she basically let me walk in with not much more than a greeting. There was a terrible quiet awkwardness that lingered.

I asked her if I could step out on the porch and have a smoke, since she was a smoker as well. I did, and she stayed inside doing nothing. She finally came outside, asked me to get up from the chair and move to a different one so she could have the one I was sitting in. An odd request I thought, but I did it anyway. We had our smoke, with little talk. We discussed dating and the Internet, etc., and I asked her why she was so desperate.

She got real pissed off at this and said she wasn't desperate at all, and that as a matter of fact, she was currently fucking the CEO of one of the largest firms in the city. Which contradicted what she had told me on the phone. She said that he was chasing after her and she wanted nothing to do with him because he was married. When we finally went back in, she looked me over and told me that I was "obese." This was news to me. I am not the cover of *Men's Health* but I am no fat bastard either. I think of myself of having kind of a Jack Black/blue collar type build with more muscle.

Then she said it was best if I left because she felt threatened by me. Mind you, I had probably said no more that two-dozen words at this point, all of which were nice, minus the desperate thing. I said that it was probably for the best since she was "crazy."

She screamed, "FUCK YOU!" and slammed the door. As I walked by her apartment from the outside she went back out to the porch for another smoke. Walking by her patio, against my better judgment, I said to her, "It's no wonder you are alone, and I hope you get used to it." Not surprisingly, she responded by yelling, "FUCK YOU, FUCK YOU! GET OUT OF HERE OR I AM GOING TO CALL THE POLICE!" Which I did not doubt because she mentioned in an earlier phone conversation that she had a restraining order against someone.

I drove home, kicking myself the whole way. What a perfect waste of a good bottle of Gatorade.

# Lesbian couple looking to experiment

We are a sexy and adventurous (mostly) lesbian couple looking to try something new. Neither of us has ever done stuff with males before, but we've decided you can't knock it until you try it. We're looking for the right guy for either a one-time nsa encounter or possibly an ongoing thing, depending on how it goes. We're open to trying lots of different stuff, within reason (no scat, etc.) but we have a few conditions.

We want everything to be mutual and go both ways, i.e. you want to do us in the back door; we get to peg you too. You want a bj; you gotta put out for us too. You want to tie us up; we get to tie you up. You get the idea. We're totally into strap-on action and various kinds of other accessories. Since we have no experience with men, we have no idea what you guys like or what feels good, but we figure with good communication this can be a mutually enjoyable experience. We will host. We might decide that once is enough, or we might decide to pursue this further, but either way it will be OUR DECISION, not yours. If this sounds interesting to you, drop an email and tell us about yourself and what your interests are.

P.S. You men seem to enjoy sending chicks pictures of your dicks. Rest assured, this will not impress us as we are LESBIANS. And furthermore, we can show you strap-ons and dildos bigger than any of you, lots of which have cool functions like vibrating and rotating and just about everything else short of making us breakfast. So do yourself a favor and send us an email with some CONTENT.

"A friend of ours actually set us up with a nice, mostly gay boy who wanted to see what women were like. He had the right attitude, we clicked, and a good time was had by all. So we ended up not needing the Internet after all for this little experiment. We received HUNDREDS of responses to our post though, lots of which almost could have been taken from the same form letter. We weren't really prepared for how daunting the deluge was going to be. We politely answered some of the first few decent emails – the (small) handful who demonstrated that they'd at least received a 6th grade education or an IQ above 45 – but after that we just couldn't keep up.

I'm sure there are plenty of guys out there who are pissed off because they took the time to write and we didn't reply (and some of them probably did deserve a considered response). But we received over five hundred emails, most of which were schlock, and we probably lost some intelligent ones in the shuffle in addition to just not having the time or the energy to respond to everyone.

I guess we sort of knew we were going to get a lot of replies, and we wrote that part at the end asking for *content* in the hope that guys would think twice before responding, and then either respond in complete sentences or not bother. But what we got was mostly confirmation that most of the male population thinks with some other organ than their brain. They should be ashamed of themselves, because they generally came across as a bunch of drooling, pathetic dorks that REALLY need to get out more. You know who you are and you best be careful – although jerking off won't give you hairy palms, you can still give yourself various types of repetitive stress injuries. (Try explaining that one to your doc!)

We do know that a threesome with a lesbian couple is every straight guy's fantasy. We know our ad sounds too good to be true, and for the vast majority of men out there it really is too good to be true because no lesbian couple would touch them with a ten-foot dildo.

Here's a hint: you don't have to tell us it's your fantasy, unless you're going to make that relevant. The more you say that makes you sound just like every other guy who manages to embody every negative straight male stereotype (social, sexual, whatever), the less we're going to want to reply to you. Incidentally, even though we're lesbians who were looking for a guy to experiment with, we're not a couple of drunken college sorority girls. We're not lace-panty-wearing bimbos who just want a jock to blow his load on our faces. You've been reading too much of your spam email. You should remember that for next time . . . if there is a next time.

Here are a few more words of advice to all the men out there who might be reading this:

1. Follow the instructions in the ad. If it says no dick pics, don't send a picture of your cock. If it asks for someone in their 20's, don't waste your time if you're 48. If it asks for content and a well-written response, don't bother responding if you're not going to use your gray matter.

2. Sending out bad pictures of yourself. Come on, guys. This one should be obvious! If the only picture you've got is uncomplimentary, don't send it! No photo is better than a butt ugly one.

Along similar lines, don't send six pictures at once. If you can avoid sending enormous file sizes, that would be nice too. Above all though, don't do your own private Calvin-Klein-inspired photo shoot alone in your room with the timer on your digital camera or with your web cam. If we thought you were a drooling dork from your email, we'll KNOW you're a drooling dork when we see that. We also don't need to see your yoga contortions such as putting your feet behind your head or sucking on your own toes from behind.

3. Spell check. So look, not everyone is a language genius. Not everyone grew up speaking English. Not everyone can remember how to spell "Wachusett." We understand this. However, you should be able to at least spell the town where you live or where you grew up. If you want to be fucked in the ass with a dildo, you should at least know that it isn't spelled 'dildoe'. If you know your spelling isn't great, consider proofing it using the spell-check tool built into your email or look it up at Dictionary.com.

(Remember that part about making first impressions?) It's kind of sad, really – so many people want to call us douche bags, but can't spell it.

4. Big words. If you don't know what it means, don't use it! If you don't know how to spell it, don't use it! If you want to sound intelligent, use words you know, and use them correctly! And by the way, if our ad piqued your curiosity, don't tell us your interest was peeked, peaked, peaqued, or piked.

5. Telling us about our lifestyle. Don't tell us you have no objections to our lifestyle, or go on about how many gay friends you have and how open-minded you are. If you were really that open-minded, you wouldn't feel the need to tell us.

As for our lifestyle, it's probably pretty similar to most people. We get up and shower in the mornings, then we go to work and make money at boring jobs that we feel fairly lukewarm about for eight hours or so, then we come home and eat dinner, maybe watch some TV or talk about politics, the economy, etc., then we go to bed. When we're in the mood we have sex, and when we're not, we don't. Sound familiar to you?

Telling us all about what you know about our lifestyle tells us that you know exactly jack, since you seem to think we're so different from everyone else.

We don't know yet whether we'll do this again or not, but in any case you guys can all stop e-mailing us now. We're not going to answer any more of you because we're not looking anymore. We're also not going to give you more details about what went on during our threesome. We wouldn't want to be guilty of giving anyone repetitive stress injuries, now would we? "

THE END

east bay press

ebp

# ABOUT THE AUTHOR

For over twenty years Thomas Kelleher worked as an advertising executive and brand strategist in Europe and the United States, creating global ad campaigns for some of the world's largest, best-known brands.

Eventually Tom decided that he needed some new challenges in life (and preserve what was left of his sanity), so he shifted gears, took a break from the ad game and focused on writing full-time. Thus his first book FREE LOVE – True Stories of Love and Lust on the Internet was born.

Originally from Washington State and a graduate of WSU, Tom's lived in Seattle where he drank lots of coffee and wore lots of flannel but still considers England his second home; where he resided next to the Queen and grew to love warm beer, woolly jumpers, fruit machines, driving on the wrong side of the road, and something called "Spotted Dick." (It's a dessert.)

He now lives in Oakland, California with his wife Laura (who he met on the Internet), baby boy William, feral cats Millie & Daisy and Super Dave The Wonder Dog.

**www.tomkelleher.com**

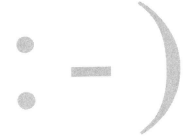

:-X